At Issue

The Right to Die

Other Books in the At Issue Series:

At Issue

The Right to Die

Jennifer Dorman, Book Editor

GREENHAVEN PRESS
A part of Gale, Cengage Learning

GALE
CENGAGE Learning

Detroit • New York • San Francisco • New Haven, Conn • Waterville, Maine • London

Christine Nasso, *Publisher*
Elizabeth Des Chenes, *Managing Editor*

© 2010 Greenhaven Press, a part of Gale, Cengage Learning.

Gale and Greenhaven Press are registered trademarks used herein under license.

For more information, contact:
Greenhaven Press
27500 Drake Rd.
Farmington Hills, MI 48331-3535
Or you can visit our Internet site at gale.cengage.com

For product information and technology assistance, contact us at

Gale Customer Support, 1-800-877-4253
For permission to use material from this text or product, submit all requests online at www.cengage.com/permissions

Further permissions questions can be emailed to permissionrequest@cengage.com

Articles in Greenhaven Press anthologies are often edited for length to meet page requirements. In addition, original titles of these works are changed to clearly present the main thesis and to explicitly indicate the author's opinion. Every effort is made to ensure that Greenhaven Press accurately reflects the original intent of the authors. Every effort has been made to trace the owners of copyrighted material.

Cover image © Images.com/Corbis.

LIBRARY OF CONGRESS CATALOGING-IN-PUBLICATION DATA

The right to die / Jennifer Dorman, book editor.
p. cm. -- (At issue)
Includes bibliographical references and index.
ISBN 978-0-7377-4684-6 (hardcover) -- ISBN 978-0-7377-4683-9 (pbk.)
1. Right to die--Popular works. 2. Euthanasia--Popular works. I. Dorman, Jennifer.
R726.R497 2010
179.7--dc22
2009048657

Printed in the United States of America
1 2 3 4 5 6 7 14 13 12 11 10

Contents

Introduction

The right to die debate focuses primarily on the legalization of physician-assisted suicide (PAS). On November 4, 2008, the state of Washington passed Initiative 1000 (I-1000), becoming the second state in the United States to legalize PAS. I-1000 states that a physician may prescribe a lethal dose of medication to a patient who meets certain criteria. The conditions include that the patient must be an adult resident of the state of Washington, be terminally ill with less than six months to live (as verified by two physicians), be mentally competent (as verified by two physicians), have made the request verbally and in writing (signed by two witnesses, at least one of whom has no ability to benefit from the patient's death), and have reiterated the verbal request a minimum of fifteen days after the initial verbal request.

The law and its safeguards are modeled after the Death with Dignity Act in Oregon, which became the first state to legalize PAS in 1994. Oregon effectively began the practice in 1997, after an initial injunction was lifted and a statute upheld through a second ballot measure. Just prior to Oregon's law taking effect, the Supreme Court ruled that there was no constitutional right to die, and turned future decisions over to the states, with Justice William Rehnquist's written opinion stating:

> Throughout the Nation, Americans are engaged in an earnest and profound debate about the morality, legality, and practicality of physician-assisted suicide. Our holding permits this debate to continue, as it should in a democratic society.

Many states have seen PAS legislation proposed, but only Oregon and Washington have had these measures pass. Although Oregon's voters may have anticipated that other states would rapidly follow, it was ten years before Washington joined them. One reason for the lack of momentum, according to Courtney Campbell in a 2008 article in *The New Atlantis*, may be that:

> Some states do not have specific laws prohibiting physician-assisted suicide; among states that do have such laws, violations may not be reported, the laws may not be enforced, or the participating provider may not be convicted or sentenced. That is to say, substantial discretion and flexibility on these questions are already embedded in the laws of many states.

Another reason may also be the moral apprehension that many feel about legalizing PAS as a form of medical treatment.

The arguments for and against PAS are not singular or simple. For many proponents the right to die is directly linked with personal autonomy, privacy, and self-determination. Others see it as a question of compassion and hope it will lead to more expansive and realistic discussions about end-of-life issues and an interest in improving quality of and access to palliative care.

For many opponents, however, there is simply no justification for helping to end a life. These absolute arguments, based in religious tradition or individual ethics, dismiss outright any possible value of PAS. But even some who might accept the practice on the basis of personal autonomy oppose it as a legal measure because of the great potential for abuse. Ending a terminally ill life is much cheaper than prolonging it, and many believe that no PAS safeguards can adequately prevent abuse. They believe that poor, disabled, and mentally ill populations are particularly at risk, and they fear a slippery slope where ultimately all people nearing death—or deemed to have a life not worth living—will feel a duty to die rather than further burdening their families and society.

Opponents of PAS also feel moral unease over asking doctors to be complicit in the act of suicide. They believe that doctors and nurses who come into the medical profession to heal should not be required to help kill. Proponents argue that doctors make these sorts of decisions all the time and could better help all of their patients if they could have this tool as a legal option. Some claim that just having the option of PAS—even if it is never used—is a comfort to those who fear agonizing pain as their illness worsens.

Before passing Initiative 1000, the citizens of Washington had the benefit of ten years of Oregon's law in practice, but this did not serve to quell the debate. Proponents claimed the law was a success and that safeguards have clearly prevented abuse, citing its relatively low use, the lack of a detrimental effect on vulnerable groups, and a positive effect on palliative care. According to Timothy Quill, writing in the *New England Journal of Medicine*, in 2007, since the introduction of the Death with Dignity Act, the terminally ill population has benefited with increases in hospice participation, pain management prescriptions, palliative care training for their physicians, and number of deaths at home as opposed to in a medical facility.

On the other hand, opponents see in Oregon all of their fears realized, pointing to insufficient reporting, little to no evaluation of patients for depression, and letters sent by health care companies stating that they will cover a lethal prescription but not potentially life-saving treatment.

The right to die and PAS legislation will certainly remain controversial; the debates show no signs of losing steam. Nicholas Kristof points out the following in a 2004 *New York Times* article:

My hunch is that the right to die will become a hotter issue over the next decade or two as baby boomers confront their own mortality. Boomers have transformed every state of life they've passed through, and they will surely transform our way of death as well.

Patients, however, will not decide this matter on their own. The future of this issue will be determined by doctors as well. According to Robert Steinbeck in a 2008 article in the *New England Journal of Medicine,*

> Physicians will continue to disagree about the wisdom of prescribing lethal doses of medication to terminally ill people who want to hasten their own deaths. Nonetheless, the approval of the Washington initiative and the potential for similar legal changes in other states provide the medical profession with an opportunity to evaluate what can be done to continue to improve care at the end of life.

The viewpoints in *At Issue: The Right to Die* explore the multifaceted arguments on both sides of the right-to-die debate. As with many complicated issues, even those on the same side of the debate do not necessarily agree on the required degree of prohibition or allowance. The highly charged issue requires that all individuals continue to explore professional, ethical, religious, philosophical, and medical issues in order to shape the end-of-life policies of the future.

1

Euthanasia Is a Rejection of God's Gift of Life

Mathew Piercy

Mathew Piercy is an intensive care specialist and anesthetist at the Royal Melbourne Hospital in Melbourne, Australia.

Euthanasia demeans the sanctity of human life. The increasing acceptance of euthanasia is the result of a tragic shift away from a biblical worldview. Modern society and popular culture promote euthanasia as compassionate, when in fact it is merely the easy and unnatural way of dealing with difficult problems such as debilitating injuries and terminal illness. It is wrong to put such power over life and death into the hands of mankind.

> 'I will neither give a deadly drug to anybody if asked for it, nor will I make a suggestion to this effect. Similarly, I will not give a woman an abortive remedy'.
>
> —*The Hippocratic Oath.*[1]

These words, penned approximately four centuries before Christ, still hold immense relevance today. Their writer was Hippocrates, a philosopher and physician of Ancient Greece who is often considered to be 'the father of medicine'. Hippocrates' 'Oath' encapsulated the idea prevalent in Greek philosophy that suicide was a social evil akin to killing another human person, but for the first time placed it in a code of practice for doctors.

Mathew Piercy, "Life: A Gift from God," *Creation Magazine*, vol. 29, June 2007, pp. 50–51. Copyright © Creation Ministries International. Reproduced by permission. creation.com/life-a-gift-from-god.

Medical students in many western countries are still required to take the above 'Hippocratic oath'. The anti-abortion clause, however, at least in my country of Australia, has been conveniently (and tragically) removed, a reflection of the secularization of our evolutionized culture. Modern medicine has all but abandoned the principle of the sanctity of human life that Hippocrates enunciated, and which is also found in the Genesis account of man being made in God's image. For example, today abortion is considered by many to be a 'pregnancy choice' rather than the destruction of another human being. Medical treatments are withdrawn from patients on the basis that they lack 'quality of life', rather than considering whether the treatment will help the person get better or preserve their life until the natural end.

The belief that we have evolved from simpler creatures is often used to justify the rejection of God as Creator and hence the rejection of His authority through His Law. Without God, life becomes purposeless. Disability, suffering and the terminal stages of life are viewed as meaningless. This is a contributing cause to the 'culture of death' that is affecting the Western world in areas such as medicine and healthcare, where people's lives are dependent on others.

The truth is that people have lost their sense of what it means to be human.

The increasing acceptance of euthanasia is part of this shift in mentality towards the 'culture of death'. Not long ago, the world watched a court of the United States rule that a disabled person, Terri Schiavo, should die by starvation and dehydration. How could an innocent person be deliberately killed in this way? (Remember that it is not like turning off complex machinery—anyone would die if prevented from taking in water or food, so we are talking about an overt act of killing the innocent—murder, by definition.)

The truth is that people have lost their sense of what it means to be human. Life, instead of being a precious gift, becomes evaluated according to its 'quality'. A person whilst young, active and productive has a high 'quality of life', yet once this person becomes old, disabled or dependent, the quality is reduced, and his or her life may no longer be considered to be worth living or protecting. Without the possibility of recovery, disability or dependence on others become grounds for the termination of that person's life.

Echoes of this sentiment were also found in Clint Eastwood's popular movie *Million Dollar Baby*. The main character, a female boxer, starts out bold and successful, but ends up suffering a high level spinal cord injury leaving her permanently disabled, dependent on a ventilator (breathing machine) and unable to move her limbs. For her, the loss of her previous abilities is too much and she seeks death, and her ventilator is switched off in what is depicted by Hollywood as a profound act of compassion. (It is interesting to note that the Third Reich used similar films to promote acceptance of euthanasia prior to the extermination of the disabled and the mentally handicapped in Nazi Germany.[2]) Far from being compassionate, the carers have simply taken the easy way out. Rather than supporting her through her illness and allowing her to adjust to life's circumstances (compare quadriplegic Christian author Joni Eareckson Tada), they assist in killing her. Such an act rejects the essential aspect that her life is not her own to take. Made in God's image, she has no right to destroy her own life, or permit others to do so, whatever her situation.

The story of Job in the Bible recounts how he refused to 'curse God and die' (Job 2:9), despite this counsel being given to him by his wife. This was because Job feared God and understood that only He has the authority to give and to take life. Even if all joy is taken out of life, as was the case with Job, that still would not justify the taking of life. Even in the depths of suffering, God's image remains, and life remains an intrinsic good, worthy of protection and support. Not to mention the fact that in rare instances, people have unexpectedly recovered from what were deemed as 'hopeless' medical situations.

When courts or individuals become the arbiters of life or death, such power in the hands of mankind (which has a poor track record on handling it wisely) is open to abuse, misjudgment, and bias.

Even in the depths of suffering, God's image remains, and life remains an intrinsic good, worthy of protection and support.

The Christian church, and indeed society in general, should never accept the lie that euthanasia represents 'a good death' (as the word's etymology[3] implies). Euthanasia, in its real sense, represents a profound rejection of the gift of life, and hence of the Giver Himself. Instead, there should be a recognition that man, being made in the image of God, has intrinsic value and dignity from conception to natural death.

The decline of respect for life in Western culture is one more symptom of the tragic foundational shift away from a biblical worldview to one based on evolutionary humanism.

References and Notes

1. As translated by Ludwig Edelstein.
2. Burleigh, M., *Death and Deliverance*, Cambridge University Press, New York, USA, p. 210, 1994.
3. From the Greek *eu* = good or easy, and *thanatos* = death.

A Compassionate God Would Not Deny Euthanasia

Hans Küng

Dr. Hans Küng, an ordained Catholic priest, was a professor of ecumenical theology at the University of Tübingen from 1960 until his retirement in 1996. He is currently the president of the Global Ethic Foundation.

Though many religious opponents to the right to die cite God's authority, nowhere did God ordain that life must be maintained in the direst of circumstances, such as extreme suffering, vegetative states, or the artificial prolonging of life in opposition to an individual's will. There are cases where the desire to die is a reasoned decision that must be respected. Strong safeguards are necessary to prevent abuse, but legalizing assisted suicide is humane and in keeping with the will of a compassionate God.

In Christian belief, human life is ultimately God's gift, and is surely not owed by Man to himself. At the same time, life according to the will of God is also Man's duty. As such it has been placed at our responsible disposal (and not [at the disposal] of others!). This holds true too for that final stage of life which is dying. Assisted death is thus to be understood as the final assistance to living, an expression—for the believer—of an autonomy grounded in theonomy [God's law].

Some say that every human being must hold out to "the ordained end" and must not give back his life "prematurely."

Hang Küng, "Assisted Death? Some Clarifying Propositions," in *Jewish Ethics and the Care of End-of-Life Patients*, edited by Joel Hurwiz, et al., Hoboken, NJ: KTAV Publishing House, Inc., 2006. Copyright © 2006 by Peter Joel Hurwitz. Reproduced by permission.

But the good Creator nowhere "ordained" the reduction of human life to purely biological and vegetative existence; the free and responsible return, under unbearable suffering, of a life definitely destroyed is not "premature." Death is not always Man's enemy.

A Living Person Is Always Human

Incurable disease, the infirmity of old age, or final unconsciousness does not turn a human being into a "nonperson" or a "no-longer-human."

This deeply humane standpoint must be espoused against certain advocates of actively assisted death, such as the Australian moral philosopher Peter Singer. It is understandable that the severely handicapped in particular react strongly against this concept (indeed, sometimes excessively against any discussion of it). Basically there is no such thing as "a life not worth living." Singer's theses require a publicly debated rebuttal.

Not in every case does the right to go on living mean a duty to do so.

Human Beings Have the Right to Die

It is because humans are human and remain so to the end, whether mortally ill (death expected in the foreseeable future) or dying (death expected shortly), that Man has the right not only to a life of human dignity but also to a humanly dignified farewell and death. The hospice movement deserves moral support and practical social promotion, for here medical endeavor and therapy have yielded the center of the stage to personal attention through conversation and to endeavors affording a dignified death.

Not in every case does the right to go on living mean a duty to do so. Quite possibly, the right to a humanly dignified death is being denied to a person through indefinite dependence on machines or medication, especially when this means existence in an irreversible vegetative state which can last hours, days, months, or years and even decades, an existence assured by pharmacological techniques of "tranquilization."

Palliative medicine, so very helpful, has made great progress and should be applied to the fullest extent. Pain therapy can render the final stages bearable for many incurably sick patients, but it is not the answer for everyone who wishes to die. Nor can pain be relieved in every case of extreme suffering. . . .

A Genuine Wish to Die

It is true that many a wish to die represents first and foremost a desire for human company, closeness, and attention. Nevertheless it is wrong and even presumptuous to disqualify every death wish as *a priori* [made without examination] a pretext. In the Medical Professional Code for German doctors, the Hippocratic Oath, totally out of date in many parts (e.g., doctors' fees), has rightly been replaced with an oath recommended by the World Medical Union that no longer makes mention of "the administration of lethal potions."

We ought to abandon the spurious argument that there is no such thing as a genuine wish to die. Such a wish indeed exists, more often than admitted by doctors or clergymen who are "ideologically" (religiously?) programmed not even to entertain such an idea. For example, an eighty-year-old woman, suffering for almost twenty years from most severe osteoporosis and enduring constant and extreme pain, writes that the wish for a quick death has been her constant companion for seventeen years, but that there is no one to help her. Aware of artificial life maintenance, many people fear a dementia lasting years or total senility.

No one should be urged to die, yet no one should be compelled to live. The decision—made out of conscience, not arbitrarily—must be left to the suffering person (or his legal representative or, possibly, a lawyer). It is presumptuous for an outsider, even a doctor, to judge whether the sufferer is being subjective in feeling that his condition is unbearable. This claim to "autonomy" on the part of the doctor gradually erodes the relationship of trust between physician and patient.

Aware of artificial life maintenance, many people fear a dementia lasting years or total senility.

Protection Against Abuse

We need clear legislative regulation, so that abuses such as manipulation by the family, social or even economic pressures can be excluded to a maximum, possibly more effectively than in the Netherlands. Abuses can never be completely prevented in any system, just as social pressure arising from increasing excessive age in our population affects every legal system. A patient's economic considerations should never be the decisive factor, but they should not be disparaged from the outset as immoral. The oft-cited relationship of trust between doctor and patient is not endangered by clearly legislated assisted death (as proved by the Netherlands), but it is endangered by the possibility, inherent in the current situation, of the physician's arbitrary disposition over my life, suffering, and death.

Assisted Suicide Is Not Murder

The Commandment "Thou shall not kill" is more precisely rendered as: "Thou shall not murder" (Exodus 20:13).

- Ending a life is murder when, and only when, it stems from base motives, malice, and violence, against the victim's will.

- Ending a life is irresponsible when the motives, though not base, are superficial and ill-considered (as when a man in his prime takes his own life because of a career fiasco, without considering his wife and children).

- Yet the ending of a life can also be responsible when happening in its due time.

Both the Bible and traditional Catholic concepts hold that "Life is, of possessions, not the highest." The idea that life is beyond our power of disposal is by no means unconditionally valid: Risking life for the sake of a higher good, individual and collective defense unto the death of the aggressor, the fatal shot which saves lives when hostages are being taken, and deploying troops at the risk of their lives—all these are regarded as morally acceptable. . . .

Middle Ground

Instead of directly or indirectly promoting extreme positions, the Churches should seek mediation between the extremes. In both the Evangelical and Catholic Church, more voices—especially medical and pastoral voices—should be expressing a reasonable middle course on contentious moral questions, and opposition to unfulfillable and inhuman maximalist demands—the irresponsible libertinism of the postmodern mood of freedom ("the unlimited right to suicide") and, at the same time, the equally irresponsible merciless rigorism [rigidity in principle or practice] based on reactionary defensiveness ("bear the unbearable as given by God, giving yourself unto God!").

He is a God of compassion, not a cruel despot desirous of seeing any human exist to his last in a hell of pain or in sheer helplessness.

To the dismay also of many Evangelical pastors and laypeople, some leaders of the German Evangelical Church are accepting, without sufficiently discriminating, the strict principles of Catholic teaching ("creeping romanization of the Evangelical Church"). No wonder that millions of people, in our republic too, are looking for religious and ethical guidance outside the major churches on questions that range from birth control to assisted death. The leaders of both churches are complaining about the increasing omission of Christian symbols and wording from death notices and about the growing number of anonymous funerals in past years: these phenomena too are related to the loss of credibility by the churches and their leadership.

A Compassionate End

When the termination of life happens in a responsible manner, let there be no mention of "murder" or even of "homicide" or "purposed killing," but rather of "assistance to die" of assistance given, in an inevitable process of dying, out of compassion and regard for the free will of the sufferer. The patient will be said to have "surrendered his life," which, when the time has come to die and the person has been properly prepared, will happen with composure and humility, in diffident [reserved] gratitude and hopeful expectation, as redelivery of life into the hands of the Creator. He is a God of compassion, not a cruel despot desirous of seeing any human exist to his last in a hell of pain or in sheer helplessness.

Once their time has come and they have been well prepared, more and more people today would like to pass away consciously. They wish for a dignified leave-taking, in an atmosphere, not of dreary hopelessness, but of spiritual comfort, accompanied to the end by doctors and caring staff, relations, and friends, with the hope of perhaps another life in a new Divine dimension, beyond time and space.

3

People Have the Right to Die with Dignity

Simon Jenkins

Simon Jenkins writes for the Guardian *and the* Sunday Times, *as well as broadcasting for the* BBC.

Recent statistics show that assisted suicide and euthanasia are taking place in hospitals throughout Britain, highlighting the need for right-to-die laws. Opportunities for reform are routinely ignored by the British Parliament, forcing decisions into the courts. The denial of the right to die is religious primitivism and undermines individual rights and personal dignity. The right to die can be legalized and regulated as well as any other difficult and complicated issue.

The Crown Prosecution Service is considering, yet again, whether to prosecute and possibly imprison otherwise law-abiding Britons for helping their loved ones to die. The parents of Daniel James, a 23-year-old rugby player crippled in a training accident, last month accompanied him to the Dignitas clinic in Switzerland, where assisted suicide is legal. In all hundred such cases so far, the director of public prosecutions has declined to act. The law is clearly unfit for purpose.

This is not regarded by parliament as a sufficient reason for changing the law. Social reform in Britain occurs not when legislators feel it appropriate but when a heart-rending case achieves mass publicity and good people launch a campaign for change. Such has been the case with laws on homosexuality, prostitution, abortion and self-defence—and perhaps one day will apply to recreational drugs. Westminster inertia always holds sway until it is overcome by an infuriated public.

There cannot be a human freedom so personal as ordering the circumstances of one's own death.

This depends on maintaining a sufficient level of fury. The James case streaked across the media horizon at the weekend, but is fading already. The CPS will probably leave it alone and another opportunity for reform will have passed. Parliament will heave a sigh of relief and return to its fascination with Corfu yachts.

There cannot be a human freedom so personal as ordering the circumstances of one's death. Yet Britain is instinctively collectivist, enveloped in prejudice, religion, taboo and prohibition. We are told how to die by the state, with no consideration for individual choice. The 1961 Suicide Act decriminalised the act of suicide, an inherently absurd diktat, but criminalised any assistance to suicide, thus making it illegal to help somebody do something legal.

The law of death is a shambles. A leading authority on euthanasia, Professor Emily Jackson of the LSE, began a recent lecture on the subject with the sensational question: "What is the most common cause of death in Britain?" Her answer was "death by killing". And who does the killing? "Doctors." One third of all registered deaths are by deliberate morphine overdose and one third by the removal of life support, premeditated acts by medical staff.

All over Britain, families gather every day of the week in hospitals and discuss with doctors how to bring a dignified death to a loved one, often in a turmoil of grief, indecision, exhaustion and shame. The near universal desire "to be allowed to die in my own home" is wilfully disregarded. Parliament's one contribution to this supreme crisis in life's journey is to threaten one and all with suits ranging from negligence to manslaughter.

The near universal desire "to be allowed to die in my own home" is willfully disregarded.

Now judges are in a position to help. Since they cannot realistically prosecute two thirds of the medical profession, nor it seems the few desperate individuals who take their relatives to Switzerland, judges are on the verge of rewriting the law. The stream of visitors to Dignitas may be breaking the law, yet the CPS has not prosecuted one.

This state of affairs is being tested in the high court by 45-year-old MS sufferer Debbie Purdy, who has asked that the DPP reveal the criteria on which he exercises his discretion over whether to prosecute, which he refuses to do. She understandably wants to know if her husband is likely to be imprisoned for taking her to Switzerland to die. Can she regard the 1961 act, as it appears, to be akin to the treason and other archaic acts, and defunct in practice?

Purdy is inviting the judicial system to do what parliament has declined to do, which is to define the reasons under which euthanasia will be allowed, if not yet regulated. In this she is supported by a YouGov poll putting support for assisted euthanasia at 86%. A poll for Dignity in Dying records 76% support, and a BMA survey of doctors 56%.

The basis on which the authorities in Switzerland, the Netherlands, Belgium and Oregon allow assisted dying varies. All require evidence of free will on the part of the dying but differ in such preconditions as the possibility of recovery, the extent of pain and the imminence of death.

None has led to an epidemic of "killings". The safeguards seem robust (compared with those governing hospitals). In more than a decade, Oregon has seen just 431 assisted deaths.

The James case, now also under judicial consideration, breaks new ground. The young man's condition was certainly not terminal and his mental state was clear. After a number of failed attempts at suicide, he expressed his wish to escape from "the prison" of his crippled body. He did not want to continue "what he felt was a second-class existence . . . in fear and loathing".

Only the most warped collectivist could argue that individuals must be kept alive against their will.

He asserted his desire to do something perfectly legal, to take his own life, but was impeded by his disability from doing so. His parents freed him from that impediment. To prosecute them would be an outrage.

Only the most warped collectivist could argue that individuals must be kept alive against their will. One anti-euthanasia lobby last week even insisted that assisted suicide "would deprive the disabled of the benefit of suicide prevention". To honour this spurious benefit, those wishing to die—and their relatives—must endure unbearable suffering at the bidding of others "for the good of society as a whole".

I wonder what kind of society that is. Perhaps it is one that used to ban pain relief in childbirth, banned abortion, and held homosexuality a sin. That this should be supported by such prominent churchmen as the archbishop of Canterbury, the archbishop of Westminster and the chief rabbi is astonishing. In years to come, their attitude will seem not just illiberal but cruel.

I might do everything I can to persuade the victim of a mortal illness or crippling injury to squeeze the last shred from whatever life still has to offer them. I might plead the example of those who have gone that extra mile and enhanced the lives of others thereby. What cannot be right is for me to deny those whose unfettered judgment has reached a wish to die, the freedom of this, the last of life's great dignities.

It is specious to claim that no safeguards can be put in place to protect against abuse. We have safeguards aplenty to regulate such risky social activities as drinking, driving, matrimony and procreation. We can draw up rules to govern the process of dying. This hangover of religious primitivism must surely end. Yet again we must turn to judges rather than members of parliament to uphold a modern liberty.

Right-to-Die Laws Would Damage Society

Margaret Somerville

Margaret Somerville is director of the Centre for Medicine, Ethics and Law at McGill University in Montreal, Canada, and author of The Ethical Imagination: Journeys of the Human Spirit.

Pleas to end an individual's suffering through assisted suicide are hard for anyone to deny, and arguments for euthanasia are easy to establish in a secular society that values individual choice above all. Arguments against euthanasia, however, are even more compelling, reaching beyond our individual interests to the responsibility we have to each other and society.

There is a trend in western democracies these days of increasing activism to legalize euthanasia and physician-assisted suicide.

Here in Canada we have seen a private member's bill (C-562) introduced in April [2008] by Bloc Québécois MP [Member of Parliament] Francine Lalonde, which would amend the Criminal Code to allow a physician to "aid a person to die with dignity."[1] So understanding the arguments both for and against these interventions is of crucial importance. But that's not necessarily easy to accomplish, if my own experience holds true more generally.

---

1. This bill did not pass.

Margaret Somerville, "The Case Against Euthanasia," *The Ottawa Citizen*, June 27, 2008. Reproduced by permission of the author.

I teach a course, "Ethics, Law, Science and Society," to upper year and graduate law students at McGill [University in Montreal, Canada] and, at the end of last semester, the topic was euthanasia.

I've researched euthanasia, physician-assisted suicide, the ethics and law of palliative care and pain relief treatment, decision-making at the end of life, and related topics, for nearly three decades and published a 433-page book, *Death Talk: The Case Against Euthanasia and Physician-Assisted Suicide.*

Yet, I came away from the class feeling that I had completely failed to communicate to most of my students what the problems with euthanasia were—that I was hitting a steel wall. This was not due to any ill-will on their part; rather, they seemed not to see euthanasia as raising major problems—at least any beyond preventing its abuse—a reaction I found very worrying.

The one student who tried to express a contrary view, although normally very articulate, ended up by saying, "Well, it's what I believe and I guess my background has something to do with that."

So, I e-mailed my students explaining I felt "that I had not done a good job in presenting the euthanasia debate ... [and] decided to see if I could work out why not by writing about it." I attached an early draft of this article and asked for comments; I received several, very thoughtful replies.

Making Sense of a Complex Issue

My concern went beyond failing to convince my students there was, at the least, a strong case to be made against euthanasia. It included the fear that their response was likely to be true also for the wider society.

The difficulty of communicating the case against euthanasia and the ease of communicating the case for it, is a serious danger, especially if, as seems likely, we are headed into another debate about whether we should legalize euthanasia in Canada.

So why is the case against euthanasia so hard to establish?

When personal and societal values were consistent, widely shared and based on shared religion, the case against euthanasia was simple: God commanded "Thou shalt not kill."

In a secular society based on intense individualism, the case for euthanasia is simple: Individuals have the right to choose the manner, time and place of their death.

In contrast, in such societies the case against euthanasia is complex. It requires arguing that harm to the community trumps individual rights or preferences.

One student explained that she thought I was giving far too much weight to concerns about how legalizing euthanasia would harm the community and our shared values, especially that of respect for life, and too little to individuals' rights to autonomy and self-determination, and to euthanasia as a way to relieve people's suffering.

She emphasized that individuals' rights have been given priority in contemporary society, and they should also prevail in relation to death. Moreover, legalizing euthanasia was consistent with other changes in society, such as respect for women and access to abortion, she said.

Legalizing euthanasia would harm the very important shared societal value of respect for life.

A Moral, Secular Argument

To respond to such arguments, we need to be able to embed euthanasia in a moral context without resorting to religion— that is, formulate a response that adequately communicates the case against euthanasia from a secular perspective.

That requires, first, countering the belief that individual rights should always prevail—a task I failed at in class.

We must show, as well, there are solid secular arguments against euthanasia; for example, that legalizing euthanasia would harm the very important shared societal value of respect for life, and change the basic norm that we must not kill one another. It would also harm the two main institutions—law and medicine—that paradoxically are more important in a secular society than in a religious one for upholding the value of respect for life. And, it would harm people's trust in medicine and make them fearful of seeking treatment.

So why now? There is nothing new about people becoming terminally ill, suffering, wanting to die, and our being able to kill them. So why now, after we have prohibited euthanasia for millennia, are we debating whether to legalize it?

Although the euthanasia debate usually centres on a dying, identified person, who wants euthanasia, I believe the answer to what has precipitated the debate lies in understanding a complex interaction of certain unprecedented changes in society. Identifying these factors can also help us to see what is needed to make the case against euthanasia clearer and stronger.

Fear of Loneliness and Death

Dying alone or unloved seems to be a universal human fear. In democratic western societies many people have a sense of loss of family and community: relationships between intimates have been converted into relationships between strangers. That loss has had a major impact on the circumstances in which we die. Death has been professionalized, technologized, depersonalized and dehumanized. Facing those realities makes euthanasia seem an attractive option and easier to introduce. Euthanasia can be seen as a response to "intense pre-mortem loneliness."

We engage in "death talk" in order to accommodate the inevitable reality of death into the living of our lives. That talk helps us to live reasonably comfortably with that knowledge, which we must do if we are still to be able to find meaning in life.

Death has been professionalized, technologized, depersonalized and dehumanized.

"Death talk" (and other morals and values talk) used to take place in religion and its churches, synagogues, mosques and temples and was confined to an hour or so a week. Today, it has spilled out into our daily lives, especially through media. The euthanasia debate is one example of such "death talk."

Moreover, "secular cathedrals"—our parliaments and courts—have replaced our religious ones. That has resulted in the legalization of societal ethical and moral debates, including in relation to death. It is not surprising, therefore, that the euthanasia debate centres on its legalization.

Aversion to Suffering

Mass media and the mediatization of societal debates, including euthanasia, also have major impact. Media focus on individual cases: People, such as Sue Rodriguez—an ALS [amyotrophic lateral sclerosis, a fatal, degenerative disease of the spinal cord] sufferer who took her fight to die to the Supreme Court of Canada—pleading for euthanasia, make dramatic, personally and emotionally gripping television.

The arguments against euthanasia, based on the harm that it would do to individuals and society in both the present and the future, are very much more difficult to present visually.

Moreover, the vast exposure to death that we are subjected to in both current-affairs and entertainment programs might have overwhelmed our sensitivity to the awesomeness of death and, likewise, of inflicting it.

But one of my students responded, "If anything, I think many of our reactions come not from an overexposure to death, but from an aversion to suffering, and an unwillingness or hesitancy to prolong pain."

Finding convincing responses to the relief-of-suffering argument used to justify euthanasia is difficult in secular societies. In the past, we used religion to give value and meaning to suffering. But, now, suffering is often seen as the greatest evil and of no value, which leads to euthanasia being seen as an appropriate response.

Might the strongest argument against euthanasia, however, relate not to death but to life?

Some answers to the "suffering argument" might include that:

- even apart from religious belief, it's wrong to kill another human;

- euthanasia would necessarily cause loss of respect for human life;

- it would open up an inevitable slippery slope and set a precedent that would present serious dangers to future generations. Just as our actions could destroy their physical environment, likewise, we could destroy their moral environment. Both environments must be held on trust for them;

- recognizing death as an acceptable way to relieve suffering could influence people contemplating suicide.

31

Might the strongest argument against euthanasia, however, relate not to death but to life? That is, the argument that normalizing it would destroy a sense of the unfathomable mystery of life and seriously damage our human spirit, especially our capacity to find meaning in life.

5

Oregon's Right-to-Die Law Has Been Successful

Ron Wyden

Ron Wyden, a Democrat, represented Oregon in the U.S. House of Representatives. He became a U.S. Senator in 1996.

The people of Oregon fought a long battle to pass the Death with Dignity Act, which made it the first state in the union to legalize physician-assisted suicide. During the time the law has been in place, safeguards have proved sufficient to prevent abuses, and end-of-life care in general has actually improved for Oregonians. As a state, Oregon has a right to make its own decisions about acceptable medical practices. Instead of criticizing Oregon, the rest of the country should focus on improving the dire state of end-of-life care by working on related issues of pain management and palliative care.

When Oregonians first adopted the Death with Dignity Act and then defended it on a second ballot initiative, they sent their government a clear message. When the American people resisted government interference in the tragic case of Terri Schiavo, they sent their government a clear message. That message is that death is an intensely personal and private moment, and in those moments, the government ought to leave well enough alone. The government ought not to attempt to override or preempt the individual's and the family's values, religious beliefs, or wishes.

Testimony of U.S. Senator Ron Wyden before the Sentate Committee on the Judiciary Subcommittee of the Constitution, Civil Rights and Property Rights, May 25, 2006.

I have testified before, and it bears repeating: I opposed physician aid in dying both as an Oregon voter and as a senator. As the former Director of the Oregon Gray Panthers[1] I witnessed first hand how many poor and vulnerable individuals receive inadequate health care. I worried primarily about the adequacy of the Oregon ballot measures' safeguards to protect the poor elderly, and as a result, I voted against the Oregon ballot measure—not once, but twice as a private citizen. Despite my personal objections, I firmly believe that my election certificate does not give me the authority or the right to substitute my personal and religious beliefs for judgments made twice by the people of Oregon. I will continue to strongly oppose any legislative or administrative effort to overturn or nullify the will of Oregon's voters on this matter.

Oregon's Lengthy Battle

Had Oregon acted hastily or without thorough examination and debate, I might not be in a position to defend the Oregon law. No one can accuse Oregonians of acting precipitously in approving the measure: The voters of Oregon did so only after two lengthy and exhaustive debates that dominated water cooler and dinner table conversation for the better part of two years.

No one can accuse Oregonians of acting precipitously in approving the [Death with Dignity Act].

The issue of physician aid in dying is settled as far as my state of Oregon is concerned. My state has endured two legal ballot initiatives, court challenges to stop the implementation of the law, attempts in Congress to overturn the law, an attempt to overturn the law through administrative action by

---

1. A public interest group that works for social change through political action.

the federal government, and, most recently, a challenge that went to the U.S. Supreme Court. Each time, the will of a majority of Oregonians prevailed.

The Death with Dignity Act

During the eight years the law has been in effect, its opponents have combed through the law looking for possible pitfalls to exploit. However, the law still stands.

During the eight years the law has been in effect, its opponents have warned there would be abuses and a stampede to Oregon. The law has not been abused. In fact, over eight years, an average of about 30 Oregonians a year have used lethal prescriptions. This, of course, is a tiny fraction of Oregonians who faced terminal illness during that time.

While I do not know how I would vote if the issue were to appear on the Oregon ballot once more, I believe it is time for me to acknowledge that my fears concerning the poor elderly were thankfully never realized, and the safeguards appear to have worked quite well in preventing potential abuses.

My fears concerning the poor elderly were thankfully never realized, and the safeguards appear to have worked quite well in preventing potential abuses.

End-of-Life Care Has Improved

What is often not discussed by opponents of the Oregon law is the Oregon Death with Dignity Act has brought about many improvements in end of life care in Oregon. Pain management has improved. My state remains the only state to discipline a physician for the under-treatment of pain. However, perhaps the most important side effect of the law is that families, health professionals and patients know they can and should have conversations about how they want to die and what their wishes are concerning treatment.

Historical Perspective

In 1997, the U.S. Supreme Court decided two important cases that should inform this discussion. The court in *Washington v. Glucksberg* and *Vacco v. Quill* rejected any constitutional right of terminally ill patients to physician aid in dying, but, equally important, the Court in those decisions left the states free to permit or prohibit assistance in dying. Indeed, the high Court encouraged states to proceed with their various initiatives in this area. Oregon has done just that.

Historically and constitutionally, states have always possessed the clear authority to determine acceptable medical practice within their borders. States are responsible for regulating medical, pharmacy and nursing practice. Even the preamble to Medicare states that "Nothing in this title shall be construed to authorize any Federal officer or employee to exercise any supervision or control over the practice of medicine or the manner in which medical services are provided. . . ."

The scientific health literature is full of studies documenting how medical practice differs from region to region, state to state and sometimes from medical institution to medical institution. End of life care should be no different.

Fair-weather friends of States' rights should be reminded that States' rights does not mean just when you think the state is right.

While other states have considered physician aid in dying since Oregon passed and implemented the Death with Dignity Act, they have not adopted it.[2] That is their choice. Yet, no one challenged their decisions in court. Neither the Congress nor the Administration attempted to overturn their decisions. Oregon's decision, reached through legal means, should be re-

2. Washington passed a similar bill in November 2008, making it the second state to legalize physician-assisted suicide.

spected as well. Fair-weather friends of States' rights should be reminded that States' rights does not mean just when you think the state is right. . . .

Pain Management Must Be Improved

I truly believe there is real common ground and that the nation would benefit if we were to focus our efforts there. All of us would like to reduce the desire and demand for physician aid in dying. In order to do that, pain management needs a huge boost, not another setback.

Previous attempts to negate Oregon's law have damaged pain management in every corner of the United States. Even the *New England Journal of Medicine* editorialized against that attempt out of concern for the impact on pain management nationwide, saying: "Many doctors are concerned about the scrutiny they invite when they prescribe or administer controlled substances and they are hypersensitive to drug-seeking behavior in patients. Patients as well as doctors often have exaggerated fears of addiction and the side effects of narcotics. Congress would make this bad situation worse."

Pain management is in a sorry state in this country. Senator [Gordon] Smith and I introduced the Conquering Pain Act to help provide families, patients and health professionals with assistance so that no patient would be left in excruciating pain [while] waiting for the doctor's office to open up.

Palliative Care Training Should Increase

The Medicare hospice benefit, created in 1987, has not been revised significantly since then. I have legislation, the Medicare Hospice Demonstration Act, to test new ways of bringing hospice benefits to the patient. For example, Medicare currently requires terminally ill patients to choose between "curative" care and hospice. In plain English, that means you can't get hospice unless you give up hope. I contend that people do not get into hospice soon enough to get its full benefits if they're forced to make such a choice. My idea, which Aetna [a health insurance provider] is currently testing, would set aside this "either/or" choice, allowing hospice to begin while the patient continues with curative care.

The nation also has a shortage of providers—physicians and nurses—trained in palliative care. Legislation I authored, The Palliative Care Training Act, provides funding to assure there is a medical faculty trained in palliative care for all ages.

It is a sad fact that not everyone can be cured. As the number of ways to prolong life multiplies, end of life care issues will be more controversial, more difficult and more painful. The aging of our population will bring more families face to face with these issues, as well. I contend that the more that is done to improve end of life care and to help support patient and family decisions, the less people will turn to physician aid in dying.

The country's legal system should not make those decisions more difficult, or more complicated.

As the number of ways to prolong life multiplies, end of life care issues will be more controversial.

Death with Dignity: Positive Outcomes

For the citizens of Oregon, the Death with Dignity Act has brought about improvement in many areas and encouraged conversations that many would never have had otherwise. For many, it has brought a small measure of peace of mind, knowing that they can remain in control of their lives if they choose to do so.

In Oregon, the end of life process has been decriminalized. And although I could not prove it, I believe in Oregon we have fewer physician aid-in-dying cases than in other states where that kind of action is prohibited. . . .

Let me close by saying that I know these are deeply personal issues for all Americans. My state has chosen a unique path. But rather than pursue a bitter and divisive debate over physician aid in dying, I would offer that we work together to make the end of life time a better one for all Americans.

6

Oregon's Death with Dignity Act Is Being Abused

Kenneth Stevens

Kenneth Stevens is vice president of the Physicians for Compassionate Care Education Foundation.

Oregon's Death with Dignity Act has done nothing to improve pain management, hospice, or palliative care, nor has it diminished the state suicide rate for nonassisted suicides. The high cost of curative treatment and the low cost of assisted suicide causes many individuals to be vulnerable under their own health care coverage. Abuse of the law is widespread, as so-called "safeguards" are not sufficient to protect against patients and doctors who use the law inappropriately.

Oregon during fall rivals states more famous for the beauty of their dying foliage, according to the [Northwest] state's official website. That claim may be contentious, but in one thing Oregon is definitely unique in the American landscape: It has a law that allows doctors to help people kill themselves.

Next month [November 2007] marks the tenth anniversary of the state's physician-assisted suicide (PAS) law. Although Oregon's Death with Dignity Act was initially approved by state voters in 1994, legal proceedings kept it from becoming operational until November 1997. The first recorded legal assisted suicide deaths began at the start of 1998. According to the Oregon Department of Human Services, which monitors the act, in the nine years from 1998 through 2006 there were 292 such deaths. Information regarding the 2007 calendar year will be released in March 2008.

The assisted suicide movement itself has acknowledged that physical pain is not the main reason for ending life. Oregon assisted suicide patients have been described by their doctors as being fiercely independent and controlling people. They fear dependency. Control and choice are the key words now used in the promotion of assisted suicide.

In the first four years (1998 to 2001) there were 91 deaths, or about 23 a year. In the last five years (2002 to 2006) there were 201 deaths, or about 40 a year. In 2006 there were 46 deaths; there were 65 prescriptions for lethal doses of secobarbital or pentobarbital written by 40 doctors.[1] Currently about one in 700 deaths in Oregon is from assisted suicide.

In 2006, there were 46 deaths; there were 65 prescriptions for lethal doses of secobarbital or pentobarbital written by 40 doctors.

Why have these Oregonians chosen to end their lives? Although the sponsors of the PAS law claimed that uncontrolled physical pain was the primary reason for legalizing assisted suicide, we have since learned that pain is not the main reason that some Oregonians have chosen it.

Less Incentive to Care

The arrival of "death with dignity" in Oregon has not created a health paradise. The national organization Last Acts issued a "report card" in November 2002 to states regarding their end-of-life care. Oregon was given a D grade for hospice care and an E grade for palliative care programs. There are concerns regarding pain management in Oregon. After four years of as-

1. In 2007 there were 49 deaths, and in 2008 there were 60 deaths, according to the Oregon Department of Human Services.

sisted suicide, an Oregon medical university study reported that there were almost twice as many dying patients in moderate or severe pain or distress as there had been prior to the law change.

Once a patient has the means to take his or her life, there is less incentive to care for the patient's symptoms and needs. A detailed report in the *American Journal of Psychiatry* in 2005 told of a depressed lung cancer patient in Oregon who had been committed to a mental hospital unit. During planning for his discharge, a palliative care consultant wrote that he probably needed attendant care at home, but providing for that additional care might be a "moot point" because he already had "life-ending medication" at home. His assisted suicide doctor did nothing for his pain and palliative care needs, but did offer to sit with him while he took the overdose. This seriously physically and mentally ill patient received poor medical advice and care because he had been prescribed lethal drugs.

Once a patient has the means to take his or her life, there is less incentive to care for the patient's symptoms and needs.

An Excuse for Rationing Care

Legitimising suicide for some can create danger for others. At a time of rising health costs administrators may build assisted suicide into their calculations. For instance, Oregon Medicaid covers the cost of assisted suicide, but not the cost of curative or local medical treatment for patients with cancer who have a less than a five per cent chance of living five years, even when that treatment can prolong valuable life. In 2003 Medicaid stopped paying for medicines for 10,000 poor Oregonians; this included patients with AIDS, those needing bone marrow transplants, people who are mentally ill and those with seizure disorders. In 2004 and the first half of 2005, an additional 75,000 Oregonians were cut from the health plan to keep the state budget balanced.

Even if an Oregon patient has Medicare or Medicaid coverage, there is limited access to health care. Sixty per cent of Oregon physicians limit or do not see Medicaid patients, and 40 per cent do not see Medicare patients. Seventeen per cent of Oregonians are without health insurance, and the share of Oregonians without health insurance has grown faster than in any other state over the past four years.

Abuse of the Law

The so-called "safeguards" in Oregon's law are meant to limit access. It is to be expected, however, that when controlling-type people—as PAS patients in Oregon allegedly are—come up against the requirements of the law, something has to give, and so the boundaries around assisted suicide in Oregon have stretched.

Many doctors are writing prescriptions for lethal drugs to patients for whom they have not previously cared, and some appear to be making it their specialty.

Some of the legal requirements are: being an Oregon resident, being mentally capable, being diagnosed with a terminal illness that will lead to death within six months, and self-administering the prescribed medication. Predictably, there are reported instances of these rules not being followed. In any case, there is no protection for the depressed or mentally ill: In recent years, only five per cent of those dying from assisted suicide had a mental health consultation. In 2006, only two of the 46 patients dying from assisted suicide were referred for psychiatric evaluation, yet depression is the most common cause of suicidal thoughts.

There are published reports about a patient diagnosed by a psychiatrist as having dementia, who still received a prescription for lethal drugs. The drug is supposed to be self-administered and ingested, and yet we have media reports of cases where that has not occurred because the patient was not capable of doing it. Other reports concern two patients whose lethal medication entered the body via a feeding tube, one of them a PEG [percutaneous endoscopic gastrostomy] tube (feeding straight into the stomach) placed for the sole purpose of taking the lethal medication. Terminally ill people are reportedly moving to Oregon from other states because of Oregon's assisted suicide law.

Many doctors are writing prescriptions for lethal drugs to patients for whom they have not previously cared, and some appear to be making it their specialty. Dr Peter Rasmussen reported that 75 per cent of the patients who come to him regarding assisted suicide are people he has never seen before. In the past four years, one doctor each year has written between six and eight prescriptions.

One thing Oregon's PAS law has not done: it has not reduced other suicides. Between 1999 and 2002 the state had a rate of suicide (not counting deaths from assisted suicide) among those 65 years of age and older that was sixth highest in the nation and one and a half times the national average.

At the same time there is no real monitoring of Oregon's assisted suicides. In the last three years the prescribing doctor was present at the time the patient took the lethal dose of sleeping drugs in only 29 of the 121 deaths. Knowledge of complications for the other 92 patients is obtained second- or third-hand. Following David Prueitt's failed assisted suicide attempt in January 2005, the state Department of Human Services (DHS) publicly stated that they had "not authority to investigate individual Death with Dignity cases—the law neither requires or authorizes investigations from DHS."

Widespread Concerns About Assisted Suicide

With majorities voting twice—in 1994 and 1997—in favor of legalization, it is unlikely that Oregon will repudiate assisted suicide in the near future. However, the [Northwest] state has failed to be the predicted harbinger of assisted suicide spreading to other states. In keeping with its geographic fringe location, Oregon represents a solitary anomaly in legalizing assisted suicide. Voter referendums and legislative bills similar to Oregon's assisted suicide law have failed in Alaska, Arizona, California, Hawaii, Maine, Michigan, Washington and Wisconsin.[2] The failure of assisted suicide extended across the Atlantic, where an Oregon-type assisted suicide bill was rejected in the British House of Lords in 2006. In early October 2007 the Washington State Medical Association rejected a proposal to be neutral in this area and strengthened its policy of opposition to PAS.

Why have PAS bills failed in other states? Because of the concern of a broad coalition of health care professionals, hospice workers, disability rights advocates, minority groups, pro-life advocates, and various moral and ethical leaders who have vigorously opposed the legalization of assisted suicides in these political jurisdictions.

They are concerned about the impossibility of containing assisted suicide once it starts; about the financial inequalities in society and about fair access to medical care by the disadvantaged. Above all, they worry that the so-called "safeguards" of Oregon's assisted suicide law are being disregarded.

2. Washington State has since passed the measure.

7

There Is No Evidence of a Slippery Slope with Right-to-Die Laws

Michael Smith

Michael Smith is the North American Correspondent for MedPage Today, *an online news source covering the medical field.*

Many euthanasia opponents claim that right-to-die laws will ultimately put vulnerable groups at risk and cause society to succumb to a moral and practical "slippery slope," wherein protective measures erode over time. However, a study published in the Journal of Medical Ethics *found no evidence of such groups— including the poor, the elderly and the physically disabled— facing heightened risks in Oregon or the Netherlands, where right-to-die laws are in place.*

Forecasts that physician-assisted suicide and euthanasia would be practiced disproportionately on vulnerable groups, such as the poor, the elderly, and women, did not prove accurate, according to researchers. . . .

The finding came from a multi-year analysis of data from Oregon, where physician-assisted suicide became legal in 1997, and [the Netherlands], where both physician-assisted suicide and euthanasia are legal, said Margaret Battin, Ph.D., of the University of Utah, and colleagues in Oregon and the Netherlands.

The researchers found no evidence that people in nine of 10 vulnerable groups died more often as a result of either physician-assisted suicide or euthanasia, they reported in the October [2007] issue of the *Journal of Medical Ethics.*

The bottom line, they said, is that there is "no current factual support for so-called slippery-slope concerns about the risks of legalization of assisted dying—concerns that death in this way would be practiced more frequently on persons in vulnerable groups."

The researchers found no evidence that people in nine of 10 vulnerable groups died more often as a result of either physician-assisted suicide or euthanasia.

AIDS patients were the only group that used doctor-assisted suicide at elevated rates, Dr. Battin and colleagues found.

"Fears about the impact on vulnerable people have dominated debate about physician-assisted suicide," Dr. Battin said. "We find no evidence to support those fears where this practice already is legal."

If anything, Dr. Battin and colleagues found, people taking advantage of doctor-assisted suicide and euthanasia tended to be slightly better off economically and better educated than average.

Evidence from Oregon and the Netherlands

In Oregon, the Death with Dignity Act allows doctors to prescribe lethal drugs to patients who have been diagnosed by two physicians as having a terminal illness [and] less than six months to live.

In [the Netherlands], the law also allows a doctor to administer the medications in what is called "voluntary active euthanasia."

Dr. Battin and colleagues found that 292 people died under the provisions of the Oregon law in its first nine years, about 0.15% of those who died in the state during that time.

In [the Netherlands], fewer than 2% of all deaths are by voluntary active euthanasia and physician-assisted suicide combined, showed 2005 mortality data on 136,000 deaths in the country.

Compared with background populations, the researchers found the elderly, women, people with low educational status, the poor, the physically disabled or chronically ill, minors, those with psychiatric illnesses including depression, or racial or ethnic minorities did not have elevated rates of doctor-assisted dying.

In Oregon, for example, 21% of all deaths occurred among people 85 or older—but only 10% of those who asked for a doctor's help were in that age category. In fact, those ages 18 through 64 were more than three times as likely to receive assisted dying as those older than 85.

Over the nine years, 46% of those who used the Oregon law were women. In the Netherlands, although the numbers fluctuated, men were generally in the majority.

In Oregon there was no sign that those without insurance were helped to die more often.

The issue of health insurance doesn't apply to [the Netherlands], where all patients have coverage, but in Oregon, there was no sign that those without insurance were helped to die more often.

Of the 292 deaths, the researchers found, there was no documented health insurance in three and insurance status was unknown in four—about 2.4%. In contrast, 16.9% of Oregon adults under the age of 65 were uninsured.

Further Findings

On the other hand, Dr. Battin and colleagues said, those with AIDS seemed to use the assisted suicide laws more often.

In Oregon, six patients with AIDS died under the act, or 2% of the total. That was 30 times the rate of those in a reference group of people with chronic respiratory disorders.

In [the Netherlands], few patients with AIDS have received a doctor's aid in dying, the researchers said. But in one Amsterdam cohort—131 men with AIDS who died before Jan. 1, 1995—22% died by euthanasia or physician-assisted suicide.

The researchers cautioned that the data from the two countries are often difficult to compare. "Where they do overlap, however, the studies are largely consistent," Dr. Battin and colleagues said.

8

Right-to-Die Laws Do Present a Slippery Slope

Rita Marker

Rita Marker is the executive director of the International Task Force on Euthanasia and Assisted Suicide.

There are many dangers inherent in legalizing assisted suicide. For example, it is certainly cheaper for a health plan to cover lethal drugs for suicide than expensive life-prolonging measures. Reports that Oregon's Death with Dignity Act has benefited patients are misleading and rely on self-reporting by doctors with little oversight. Safeguards cannot be strong enough to fight the pull of economics. Regardless of what proponents say, continuing to legalize assisted suicide will lead our society down a deadly path to cost containment.

Oregon seems to have found a surefire way to lower health care costs: Tell the patient you'll pay for drugs that will end her life, but not those that would extend her life. Here's how it works:

In May 2008, 64-year-old retired school bus driver Barbara Wagner received bad news from her doctor. She found out that her cancer, which had been in remission for two years, had returned. Then, she got some good news. Her doctor gave her a prescription that would likely slow the cancer's growth and extend her life. She was relieved by the news and also by the fact that she had health care coverage through the Oregon Health Plan.

It didn't take long for her hopes to be dashed.

Barbara Wagner was notified by letter that the Oregon Health Plan wouldn't cover her prescription. But the letter didn't leave it at that. It also notified her that, although it wouldn't cover her prescription, it would cover assisted suicide.

After Wagner's story appeared in the Eugene *Register-Guard*, the Oregon Health Plan acknowledged that it routinely sends similar letters to patients who have little chance of surviving more than five years, informing them that the health plan will pay for assisted suicide (euphemistically categorized as "comfort care"), but not for treatment that could help them live for months or years.

Certainly, spending $100 for deadly drugs is cost effective. And, ever since the Oregon Death with Dignity Act transformed the crime of assisted suicide into a "medical treatment" more than ten years ago, it has been perfectly legal. Oregon doctors prescribe lethal overdoses of drugs. Pharmacists dispense them, sometimes with instructions to "take all of this with a light snack and alcohol to cause death." Patients die after taking them.

> *Barbara Wagner was notified by letter that the Oregon Health plan wouldn't cover her prescription. But ... it would cover assisted suicide.*

Seeking a Similar Law in Washington State

Now, an Oregon-style law is under consideration in Washington state. After engineering passage of Oregon's Death with Dignity Act, assisted-suicide advocacy groups thought other states would rapidly adopt similar laws. But they were wrong. Because their attempts to pass Oregon-style laws in more than twenty states failed, the Portland-based Death with Dignity National Center (DDNC), along with Compassion & Choices (the former Hemlock Society), devised a plan in 2005 called "Oregon plus One" to break the logjam. It is based on the premise that, if just one more state follows Oregon's lead, then other states will fall in line.

The plan was put into effect in early 2006. In its 2007 annual report, the DDNC noted that it had spent a year "researching and collecting data to determine that state which is most likely to adopt a Death with Dignity law. . . . Through these efforts we have identified Washington as the state." (Note that the assisted-suicide group chose Washington. Washingtonians were not in on the selection.)

After choosing Washington as the target state, the DDNC reported, "[W]e have never had such great odds of success as we have in Washington in 2008. That is why we will be directing $1.5 million over the next year and a half to the efforts. . . . Our organization is providing leadership, political strategy, and financial resources to this monumental effort."

The political campaign was formally announced in late 2007 and, in mid-July 2008, Initiative 1000 (called the "Washington Death with Dignity Act," a measure virtually identical to Oregon's law) qualified for the 2008 general election ballot.[1] Its advocates contend that Oregon's ten-year experience demonstrates that a Death with Dignity law not only works well, but is actually a benefit to patients. As proof they point to Oregon's annual official reports, to the law's "safeguards," and to studies in professional journals.

Claims of Oregon's Success Are Misleading

However, their claims are at best misleading. For example, under Oregon's law doctors participating in assisted suicide must file reports with the state. So the only physicians providing data for official annual reports are those who actually prescribe lethal drugs for patients. First, they help the person commit suicide and, afterwards, they report whether their ac-

1. The state of Washington passed an assisted-suicide law in November 2008.

tions complied with the law. Then, that information is used to formulate the state's official annual reports. However, according to *American Medical News*, Oregon officials in charge of issuing the reports have conceded that "there's no way to know if additional deaths went unreported." (The official number of reported assisted-suicide deaths in Oregon is 341.)

Indeed, the official summary accompanying one annual report noted that there is no way to know if information provided by the physicians is accurate or complete. But, it stated, "[W]e, however, assume that doctors were being their usual careful and accurate selves." The reporting agency also acknowledged that it has no authority or funding to investigate the accuracy of those self-reports.

It would be nifty if the Internal Revenue Service allowed such unverified and unverifiable self-reporting.

Oregon's Safeguards Are Insufficient

The Oregon law's safeguards are equally problematic. They contain enough loopholes to drive a hearse through them. The safeguards certainly do have the appearance of being protective. They deal with requests for assisted suicide, family notification, and counseling or psychological evaluation. However, those safeguards are about as protective as the emperor's new clothes:

- The oral requests, which must be separated by fifteen days, do not need to be witnessed. In fact, they don't even have to be made in person. They could be made by phone—even left on the physician's answering device. The written request must be witnessed, but it could be mailed or faxed to the doctor.

- The law states that the physician is to "recommend that the patient notify next of kin," but family notification is not required. It is entirely possible that the first time family members find out that a loved one was contemplating suicide could be after the death has occurred.

- Doctors can facilitate the suicides of mentally ill or depressed patients without any prior counseling being provided. A psychiatric evaluation is required only if the physician believes that the mental illness or depression is causing impaired judgment. According to Oregon's latest official report, not one patient who died after taking the lethal drugs was referred for counseling prior to being given the prescription.

It is entirely possible that the first time family members find out that a loved one was contemplating suicide could be after the death has occurred.

Additionally troubling are omissions in both Oregon's law and the Washington proposal. For instance, doctor shopping is not prohibited. If one physician refuses to prescribe assisted suicide because, for example, the patient is not competent to make an informed death request, that patient or a family member can go from doctor to doctor until finding one who will write the prescription.

Moreover, neither Oregon's law nor Washington's proposal has any type of protection for the patient once the prescription is written. While the requests for assisted suicide are to be made knowingly and voluntarily, there is no provision that the patient must knowingly and voluntarily take the lethal drugs. Dr. Katrina Hedberg, the lead author of most of Oregon's official reports, acknowledged that there is no assessment of patients after the prescribing is completed. She said that the "law itself only provides for writing the prescription, not what happens afterwards."

Forcing Physicians to Lie

The Washington proposal, in a major departure from Oregon's law, adds a layer of unprecedented deception by forcing doctors to lie about the cause of death. It requires that, when a patient dies after taking the prescription for assisted suicide, the physician "shall list the underlying terminal disease as the cause of death." Washington State Medical Association president, Brian Wicks, M.D., described the requirement in a WSMA press release opposing the initiative:

> Under I-1000, if a physician prescribes a lethal overdose, when that physician completes the death certificate, he or she is required—actually required—to list the underlying disease (say lung cancer) as the cause of death, even when the doctor knows full well that the patient died due to the suicidal overdose he or she prescribed. To my knowledge there's no other situation in medicine in which the death certificate is deliberately falsified—and in which this falsification is mandated by law.

Studies Can Be Misleading

Concerns about assisted suicide often are thrust aside by citing studies to bolster the benign nature of legalized assisted suicide. Such studies are often far from unbiased as indicated by one that was released in late 2007, just as the Washington campaign formally got underway. Published in the *Journal of Medical Ethics*, and widely reported in news articles across the country, it concluded that assisted suicide in Oregon is abuse free, even for vulnerable people. (The basis for that conclusion was an examination of Oregon's official annual reports.) Its principle author was Margaret Pabst Battin. Battin, a University of Utah philosophy professor, is a longtime supporter of assisted suicide and a member of DDNC's advisory board—information not disclosed in either the journal article or the initial flurry of national media coverage.

Thus, the "proof" for the benign nature of legal assisted suicide—found in official annual reports, safeguards and studies—is preposterous. Assisted-suicide advocates take great umbrage when this is pointed out, as they do at any suggestion of assisted-suicide being used for cost containment. Do assisted-suicide advocates intend this as a cost-containment measure? Does it matter? Did their intentions mean anything to Barbara Wagner? Or does it really come down to recognizing that, even if its advocates don't intend to follow such a path, the force of economic gravity inevitably leads in this direction?

Concerns about assisted suicide often are thrust aside by citing studies to bolster the benign nature of legalized assisted suicide. Such studies are often far from unbiased.

When all is said and done, it is not the intent of assisted-suicide supporters that matters. Instead, it is the law's deadly content and the inevitable price that we would all pay for health care cost containment—Oregon style.

9

Physician-Assisted Suicide Has No Place in Palliative Care

José Pereira, Dominique Anwar, Gerard Pralong, Josianne Pralong, Claudia Mazzocato, and Jean-Michel Bigler

The authors of this article are all palliative care physicians in Switzerland.

Assisted suicide and euthanasia go against the basic directive of palliative care, which is to provide care and comfort to those facing the end of life. The legalization of these practices poses several risks for palliative care units. These risks include causing palliative staff members to face stressful personal and professional conflicts; confusing the public about the purpose of palliative care; and turning palliative care units into dumping grounds for assisted suicide cases. Regardless of existing or future legalization, assisted suicide and euthanasia must remain outside the purview of palliative care.

Euthanasia or physician-assisted suicide (PAS) [has] been legalized in a small number of jurisdictions. Oregon allows PAS, while in the Netherlands both PAS and euthanasia are legal. Belgium permits euthanasia and Luxembourg may follow suit. Although euthanasia is illegal in Switzerland, assisted suicide is allowed and may be performed by nonphysicians.

In January 2006 the Centre Hospitalier Universitaire Vaudois (CHUV) in Lausanne became the first university hospital

José Pereira, Dominique Anwar, Gerard Pralong, Josianne Pralong, Claudia Mazzocato, and Jean-Michel Bigler, "Assisted Suicide and Euthanasia Should Not Be Practiced in Palliative Care Units," *Journal of Palliative Medicine*, vol. 11, no. 8, 2008, pp. 1074-1075.

in Switzerland to allow, under exceptional circumstances, assisted suicide within its walls. Staff members, however, are not obliged to provide assisted suicide. In such circumstances, external persons, including members of right-to-die societies, are called in. In early 2007, The Hôpitaux Universitaires of Geneva (HUGE), made a similar decision. Other hospitals in the cantons of Vaud and Geneva are considering instituting similar policies. Current and future palliative care units in these hospitals would therefore be placed in a situation of conforming to these institutional directives. We defend the position that assisted suicide (and euthanasia) should not be allowed in palliative care units because it would place many units, their staff and, in some cases, their patients and families, in untenable positions.

Reasons for Not Allowing Assisted Suicide or Euthanasia in Palliative Care Units

Intentionally hastening death is contrary to palliative care philosophy. The World Health Organization's definition states that palliative care does not intentionally hasten death. Most regional, national, and international palliative care organizations and societies have adopted this position. Several reasons are given to justify this stand, amongst which are the beliefs that these practices are intrinsically wrong, violate professional integrity and may endanger the relationship with the patient. Offering assisted suicide (or euthanasia) within palliative care units would therefore mean the endorsement of a policy that runs counter to international norms and standards of palliative care practice.

Sends mixed message to a public that is already poorly informed about palliative care. Many members of the public are unaware of palliative care or misinformed about what it represents. Only 30% of the Canadians could explain what it represented in a 1997 study. In a British study, only 18.7% of patients referred to a palliative care service could adequately define the term "palliative care." Allowing assisted suicide and euthanasia within palliative care units, even if the units' staff members are not directly involved in the practices, would send mixed messages to a public that is already misinformed about palliative care.

The World Health Organization's definition states that palliative care does not intentionally hasten death.

Source of distress for some patients and families. Not all members of the public endorse assisted suicide or euthanasia. Patients and families who disagree with assisted suicide or euthanasia may decline admissions to palliative care units for fear of being subjected, either directly or indirectly, to these practices. For some patients, the availability of assisted suicide or euthanasia on a palliative care unit may erode their trust in the unit and the treatments it offers.

Source of tension and conflict between palliative care staff. Health care professionals are divided on the issue of assisted suicide and euthanasia. Although the extent of this division varies from country to country, at least a third to a half of physicians or nurses polled express opposition to or support of the practices. Opposition to these practices is particularly strong amongst palliative care professionals; 92% of members of the United Kingdom Association for Palliative Medicine and approximately 72% of physicians of the Swiss Palliative Care Society do not support the legalization of PAS or euthanasia. However, a small minority are open to its legalization (18% in Switzerland). These sentiments may mirror the position of [T.E.] Quill and [Margaret] Battin [co-editors of the book *Physician-Assisted Dying: The Case for Palliative Care & Patient Choice*], who contend that while good palliative care should be a standard of care for those who are dying, strong philosophical and ethical principles support access to PAS as a last resort in those rare circumstances where suffering becomes intolerable despite the best palliative care possible.

These contrasting values and views may result in significant tension and conflict between staff members should assisted suicide or euthanasia be allowed on a palliative care unit if not all team members are of the same opinion. [L.] Wilkes and colleagues, for example, have described how varying views in a palliative care team towards these practices resulted in unresolved tensions that affected their relationship with patients and each other.

Health care professionals are divided on the issue of assisted suicide and euthanasia.

Source of personal distress for some staff members. Staff members with strong or even ambivalent views towards assisted suicide or euthanasia may find themselves in a dilemma. Hospice nurses and social workers in an Oregon-based study reported conflict between their personal beliefs against PAS and their advocacy for patient autonomy. The biggest dilemma arose from the conflict between two important hospice values: honoring patient autonomy versus promoting a death experience in which personal and spiritual transformation are possible. They reported other sources of distress, including a sense of "failure" if their patients ultimately chose to hasten death by PAS, conflicts over whether helping patients redefine quality of life impinges on their autonomy, and conflicts over whether to advocate for the patient when the family is against it. Several subjects felt that they had been drawn into an assisted suicide to a greater extent than they would have liked.

[Writer K.R.] Stevens has highlighted the adverse psychological and emotional effects on some physicians who have participated in euthanasia and/or PAS. Caring for terminally ill patients on a daily basis can, at times, be emotionally taxing. The emotional effects of participating directly or indirectly in assisted suicide, particularly when it runs against one's values, may add additional burden. Professionals who do not support the practice may feel torn between nonabandonment and complicity if patients ask them to be present during the final act.

Places palliative care teams in the position of gatekeepers. Allowing assisted suicide or euthanasia on palliative care units could place the team in a position of gatekeepers for assisted suicide. The team, for example, may be drawn into mediating between a patient who has requested assisted suicide and a family that disagrees with the request.

A decision to proceed with assisted suicide or euthanasia may halt attempts at addressing the underlying problems.

Dynamics of care altered once decision made to proceed with assisted suicide or euthanasia. The reasons that prompt patients to request hastening of death are often complex. The wish to hasten death may also fluctuate. Responding to these underlying problems requires a combination of time, the appropriate interprofessional expertise, and therapeutic relationships between caregivers and patients. A decision to proceed with assisted suicide or euthanasia may halt attempts at addressing the underlying problems. Anecdotal evidence suggests that the dynamics of care may change once patients make a final decision to proceed with assisted suicide or euthanasia. The focus changes to making practical preparations for receiving assisted suicide or euthanasia. This can derail the team's efforts to ameliorate the sources of distress.

Palliative care units may become "dumping sites" for assisted suicide (or euthanasia). Access to a palliative care unit that allows assisted suicide or euthanasia may prompt some hospital teams to transfer patients with such requests to the palliative care unit rather than be burdened with having to deal with the requests themselves.

Possible Negative Consequences of Excluding Assisted Suicide

It would be important to consider the possible negative consequences of disallowing assisted suicide or euthanasia in palliative care units. The specialized interprofessional competencies that these units provide is often the very expertise that is required to address the reasons underlying patients' requests for assisted suicide. A policy that excludes assisted suicide in these units may prevent some of these patients from being admitted and receiving care that could result in them rescinding their original requests. Patients whose wishes for assisted suicide (or euthanasia) despite palliative care will have to be transferred out of the unit again. This may be perceived as abandonment by patients and families. Professionals in the units patients are transferred to may feel unfairly burdened. One strategy to address this potential problem would be to inform patients early on in the relationship that the team does not provide assisted suicide or euthanasia. This would allow them to decide whether or not to continue the relationship or to seek other kinds of support.

The Risks Are Too Great

Allowing assisted suicide or euthanasia in palliative care units or hospices is associated with considerable risks. Notwithstanding the respective strengths of the arguments for and against assisted suicide or euthanasia, not including these practices as part of palliative care would seem the most prudent approach at this time. This should not however stop an ongoing constructive and mutually respectful discourse between those against assisted suicide and euthanasia and those in favour of these practices. In jurisdictions that allow assisted suicide or euthanasia, palliative care units should be exempted from allowing assisted suicide and euthanasia. As long as the moral permissibility of assisted suicide or euthanasia remain open questions, palliative care units must be permitted to stand outside of the debate, where they can focus on providing care and comfort for patients approaching death. This stand has recently been supported by the CHUV's administration.

10

The Right to Die May Be an Important Part of End-of-Life Care

Timothy Quill

Timothy Quill is a Professor of Medicine, specializing in palliative care, at the University of Rochester Medical Center. He is the author of five books that deal with end-of-life issues, including The Case for Physician-Assisted Dying: The Case for Palliative Care & Patient Choice.

In recent years, palliative care has made strides in program quality, treatment options, and access to services. There are, however, [individuals] whose suffering cannot be sufficiently relieved with existing methods. It is difficult to say whether physician-assisted death, as in the ability of a doctor to give a lethal prescription, should be one of the last-resort alternatives included in palliative care, but with proper safeguards, this may be an important option for some individuals.

Although there has been relatively little activity in the last ten years with regard to legal access to physician-assisted death, this fall [2008] a citizens' initiative in the state of Washington is proposing an Oregon-style law that would allow legal access to potentially lethal medication for terminally ill pa-

Timothy Quill, "Physician-Assisted Death in the United States: Are Existing 'Last Resorts' Enough?" *The Hastings Center Report*, vol. 38, no. 5, September/October, 2008, pp. 17–22. Copyright © 2008 Hastings Center. Reproduced by permission.

tients, subject to defined safeguards.[1] As the rhetoric inevitably heats up, this seems like a good time to review areas of progress in palliative and end-of-life care and to consider whether laws like the one on the table in Washington are either needed or desirable.

Several things are clear: (1) Palliative care and hospice have improved in terms of access and delivery, and they remain the standards of care for addressing the suffering of seriously ill patients. (2) Despite state-of-the-art palliative measures, there will remain a relatively small number of patients whose suffering is insufficiently relieved. (3) Several "last resort" options, including aggressive pain management, forgoing life-sustaining therapies, voluntarily stopping eating and drinking, and sedation to unconsciousness to relieve otherwise intractable suffering, could address many of these cases. The question remains as to whether physician-assisted death—that is, providing terminally ill patients with a potentially lethal prescription that they could ingest on their own to relieve otherwise intractable suffering by directly hastening death—should be one of these last-resort options.

My own answer to this last question is a cautious "yes": open access to physician-assisted death, subject to the safeguards of excellent palliative care and access to other last-resort options, gives patients an important additional option, and the benefits of legalization outweigh the risks. . . .

Excellent Palliative Care Must Come First

All last-resort options, including physician-assisted death, make sense only if excellent palliative care is already being provided. Mandatory palliative care consultation should therefore be a standard safeguard for any and all of these practices. Over the next ten years, medical institutions and professional groups should ensure that all clinicians who care for seriously

1. Washington State passed Initiative 1000 on November 4, 2008, making it the second State to legalize physician-assisted suicide.

ill patients are competent in the basics of palliative care and that specialty-based palliative care consultation is available for the more challenging cases.

There is also a need to develop explicit, predictable strategies to respond to difficult clinical situations where patients experience severe suffering despite state-of-the-art palliative care. Many of these patients will benefit from a discussion and exploration of last-resort options that may or may not include physician-assisted death. There are two main clinical situations in which this might come up:

All last-resort options, including physician-assisted death, make sense only if excellent palliative care is already being provided.

Patients who are worried about future suffering and wonder what options would be available to them. This conversation begins with an exploration about hopes, fears, and prior experiences of family and friends. Such patients frequently want to know what options they could have in the future if their suffering becomes unacceptable to them. In response to these inquiries, the clinician should talk to the patient about how he or she approaches such situations and what last-resort options could be provided if needed. Many patients are reassured by learning about options other than physician-assisted death and by the willingness of the clinician to explore this domain and to commit to working with them and addressing their suffering throughout the illness until death. They can then be free to spend their remaining time and energy on other important personal and family matters.

Patients who eventually experience suffering that is unacceptable to them. This is a much smaller population than those who are worried about the future, but these patients' needs can be more challenging. The starting point is always to explore the patient's suffering in its totality, including why it is now experienced as unacceptable. Part of this assessment is to ensure that standard palliative care is being skillfully applied, and that the request does not emanate from anxiety or depression that might be otherwise addressed. A second opinion by a specialist in palliative care should be obtained. If there are no good alternatives, then the last-resort options that are legally available should be explored in the approximate order presented in this paper. Usually, but not always, options other than physician-assisted death will adequately address the patient's clinical situation and be acceptable to the patient. In the event that no other possibilities are workable or acceptable, physician-assisted death would need to be considered in light of the legal environment (the approach in Oregon will be very different than the rest of the country) and the values of patient, family, and clinician.

Will Physician-Assisted Death Be Necessary?

Some patients will prefer access to physician-assisted death even if the other last-resort options are predictably available. Patients who request and eventually act using physician-assisted death in Oregon have a strong interest in controlling their fate, and physician-assisted death puts more choice directly in their hands. However, all the last-resort options, including physician-assisted death, are imperfect. Although each addresses some situations particularly well, there are other situations where they would not be as helpful.

For example, voluntarily stopping eating and drinking has the advantage of putting the decision in the patient's hands, but it requires tremendous discipline not to drink if one is thirsty and capable of drinking, and the duration of the process is too long if symptoms are severe and immediate. On the other hand, medical sedation to unconsciousness may be very frightening to those who value consciousness and being in charge, and there is no way to verify that the sedated patient is not still suffering but unable to report it. Finally, physician-assisted death requires that the patient be physically capable of self-administration and able to swallow a concentrated amount of lethal medication. In addition to these practical issues, any of these options may be morally troubling for patient, family, physician, or staff.

Adding physician-assisted death to the list of last-resort options has both risks and benefits. One benefit is that it adds another important possibility for terminally ill patients who experience unacceptable suffering. We should be as responsive as possible to these patients without violating fundamental values, but it is clear that the patient's values in this context count the most, followed by the family and then the clinician (if the course of action requires the physician's participation). Most patients will be reassured by the possibility of an escape, and the vast majority will never need to activate that possibility. But some patients will need a way out, and arbitrarily withholding one important option from patients whose options are so limited seems unfair.

The last-resort options other than physician-assisted death must become more standardized, available, and accountable.

The main risk of including physician-assisted death with other last resort options is that it seems to be very polarizing in the United States, where there is wide agreement about palliative care and hospice being the standards of care and also a surprising level of acceptance of the other last resort possibilities. Even the Supreme Court, in its 1997 decision, made it clear that "obtaining medication . . . to alleviate suffering even to the point of causing unconsciousness and hastening death" is legally acceptable. Opponents of physician-assisted death may work to further restrict access or even prohibit access to other last-resort alternatives as they become more well known and predictably available.

On the Horizon

It seems highly likely that palliative care and hospice will continue to expand in the United States and other Western countries. There are very few places in the health care system where we can simultaneously save money and improve quality, but palliative care and hospice have the potential to do both. On the quality side, improvements in pain and symptom management, more informed medical decision-making, and enhanced patient and family support are core elements of palliative care and hospice. The cost savings will come not from restricting access to expensive treatments and technologies, but from a better informed consent process for patients and families concerning medical treatments with marginal benefit and coordinated care for patients with very complex treatment. Hospice continues to be the gold standard for end-of-life care, but its challenge is to design programs that would allow patients to simultaneously continue some disease-directed therapies in order to serve a wider range of dying patients. If these programs can be proven cost-effective, then perhaps the hospice benefit can be expanded, and hospice and palliative care could be better integrated into traditional medical care. Palliative care needs to be part of the standard of care for all seriously ill patients, whether or not they choose to continue disease-directed therapy in any form.

The last-resort options other than physician-assisted death must become more standardized, available, and accountable. There is currently too much variation. Some patients may be denied access to them because clinicians or institutions are reluctant to use them, while at the same time, others are given last-resort options when more standard palliative measures would have been more appropriate. Better policies and procedures should begin at the national level, with local programs following suit. Fortunately, medicine seems to be moving in this direction. Witness a recently published American Medical Association guideline [in *American Medical News*, July 7, 2008] on sedation to unconsciousness that is consistent with position statements by the American Academy of Hospice and Palliative Medicine and others.

Similar guidelines and policies are needed for voluntarily stopping eating and drinking. Because these options are intended to be rarely used, all institutions should review their own practices against the position statements of leadership organizations. For example, my institution has a guideline on sedation to unconsciousness for treatment of refractory [unmanageable] suffering, and we review every single case in which it is utilized. The state of California is considering a law entitled the California Right to Know End-of-Life Options Act,[2] which requires that patients be given information about both hospice and last-resort options, should they request it. The goal of all these initiatives is to improve predictable access and accountability both for hospice/palliative care and for legally permitted last resort options.

Although some proponents of physician-assisted death will find the incremental, state-by-state approach to legalization frustrating, it has some value.

State by State Approach

In the domain of physician-assisted death, the most pressing change on the horizon is the Oregon-style citizens' initiative in the state of Washington. Residents of the state are already relatively well educated on the subject, having been through an unsuccessful initiative in 1991, and they are more aware of the Oregon experience, being adjacent geographically and relatively similar demographically. Citizens' initiatives begin by gathering signatures of support from a large number of residents. If the legally determined threshold is achieved, the initiative is then placed on the ballot during the next election

---

2. The Act passed and was signed into law in September 2008.

cycle and subject to the popular vote. Not all states sanction citizens' initiatives, but in my opinion, they are more likely to be successful in legalizing physician-assisted death than legislative approaches, given the relatively high level of public support and the tendency for the issue to get polarized in legislative situations. Nonetheless, legislative processes to legalize physician-assisted death were recently attempted in California, and before that there were near misses in Hawaii and New Hampshire.

Although some proponents of physician-assisted death will find the incremental, state-by-state approach to legalization frustrating, it has some value. For one thing, it gives us time to study the intended and unintended effects of legalization before national implementation. We can simultaneously evaluate the impact of better and more widespread access to hospice and palliative care, and of more predictable and accountable availability of other last-resort options. In addition, it keeps the movement a grass-roots one—particularly when it happens through citizens' initiatives. That may not make the practice of physician-assisted death less controversial, but it can perhaps make the process through which physician-assisted death is legalized less controversial.

11

Assisted Suicide Is a Valid Medical Decision

Alois Geiger

Alois Geiger is a physician at the Dignitas Center in Switzerland.

Physician-assisted suicide is a compassionate option for those who suffer and have reached a clear decision to end their lives peacefully. While suicide is not the preferred way to end life, it is a perfectly reasonable option. Physicians are in the unique position of being able to prescribe medication that can, in worst cases, make such a peaceful end possible.

Dignitas[1] is a good thing, Exit[2] of course too. What do you think about this? I know what I am talking about because I am one of the doctors who writes prescriptions for members of Dignitas. A prescription for what? A prescription that allows the person in question to end his life in a pain-free way, free of brutality, and moreover to do so not alone but accompanied by people standing lovingly at his side.

I know that many people disapprove of my activities. These people are convinced that no individual has the right to determine the end of his life. They are also sure that a doctor should never prescribe a medication to end life because he is professionally obliged to save life. The Hippocratic oath is what they have in mind.

1. An assisted suicide facility in Switzerland.
2. An international assisted suicide information and advocacy organization based in Australia.

Alois Geiger, "Why I Prescribe Drugs for Suicide," *Times Online*, October 24, 2008. Copyright © 2008 Times Newspapers Ltd. Reproduced by permission.

The Hippocratic Oath Today

We doctors today do not swear this oath and there is a reason for that—it is largely out of date. For example it forbids the surgical removal of a bladderstone, a sensitive issue in the old days. Today every surgeon can perform this operation without a problem.

The oath also forbids giving abortive medication to a pregnant woman. This used to be a risky matter for mothers because their pregnancies were usually well advanced before the foetus was detected. Nowadays an effective and safe drug can end a pregnancy in the early weeks without a problem. The excision of bladderstones is not immoral and the same can be said for a socially approved termination of pregnancy administered by a doctor.

When it comes to prescribing medication to a patient to help end his life, I view the Hippocratic oath in a similar way. With sodium pentobarbital, NaP, we have a drug that gives us for the first time the possibility of allowing a person to swiftly and gently pass away.

> *The social rejection of suicide does not so much derive from the Hippocratic oath but rather from Christian traditions.*

Religion Is the Biggest Obstacle

And what if there is no God?

The social rejection of suicide does not so much derive from the Hippocratic oath but rather from Christian traditions. Suicide is abhorred by all monotheistic religions. The Christian religion, which has influenced most of us, trusts to God's will in all of life's difficult moments. Only God who gave us life is entitled to take it away, runs the argument. So suicide becomes a sin. But what if this God doesn't exist? For those who do not believe, can there not be arguments for deciding the end of one's life: a life of suffering perhaps, or one blighted by increasing isolation, or the dependency on outside care?

When Is Assisted Suicide Reasonable?

Certainly committing suicide can be pointless. And killing oneself without outside help is always uncertain and usually a violent way of ending life. A suicide does not make sense if it is prompted by a lack of life experience: love sickness for example, financial problems or other accumulated minor woes that have been blown up out of proportion by one's own ego.

How does it look though when an illness occupies more and more space in one's life or when life is coming rapidly to a close . . . ? Or when one's despair is so enduring that even long-term psychiatric help cannot give real assistance?

Should one not be allowed to make use of medical means to release oneself from suffering? The wish to commit suicide is most understandable when it develops over time, rather than overnight.

Only a doctor with a medical practice can prescribe strong sleeping medication. For me there is no question about writing such a prescription in a tragic situation, knowing that it cannot help his illness but will help him realise his wish for a self-determined suicide.

The wish to commit suicide is most understandable when it develops over time, rather than overnight.

In my experience with would-be suicides it is practically always the case that the mere act of writing out the prescription evokes a sense of great relief in the patient: "At last someone understands me and is ready to help in the way I want. Others want to persuade me that my life is worth living at any cost. But I know better." That is what they say.

Naturally I would rather help a person in a traditional medical way. Sadly that is only rarely the case because I am not a Super-Doctor who can second guess the many medical authorities already consulted by the patient. But I always receive the gratitude of the sick person when I give him the prescription. At that moment they know that they can get something almost unobtainable elsewhere in the world—a suicide, without legal repercussions, accompanied by people, mostly close family.

A Doctor's Obligation

The other day a patient came to me suffering from a spreading neurological disease that was increasingly paralysing his muscles. He lived alone, had no family responsibilities. As a doctor I have seen many people in worse conditions and who nonetheless were ready to carry on living with their suffering and disabilities. Is it my right, or even my duty as a doctor to turn down a prescription for NaP for this man and make it very difficult for him to end his life—just because somebody in a similar situation is prepared to live longer? Does the opinion of other people overrule one's own sense of worth?

Just now, there was another conversation with him. He is not wheelchair-bound yet. With a stick he can still climb a few stairs. He is missing everything that he has lost through illness—his career, his walking, climbing, driving a car. He will not be able to take care of himself much longer, already depends on outside help. And there is the rub—he does not want to be ever more dependent on other people.

It is my duty as a doctor to tell him that there is no shame in being dependent on others, that he should see the good sides of life. I should tell him that everything would change if he could only see that the bottle is half full not half empty. Is it really my duty to treat him like a child in that I deny him the prescription? He needs me for that slip of paper. Is it correct to deny him the indisputably most humane means to determine the end of his life? If I do not help him, do I not play God, taking away from him the option of a gentle and, in his eyes, a rational death?

Mental Health

Someone who does not want to live is seen as clinically ill. He is labelled a depressive and sent to a psychiatrist. Often a psychiatrist really can help. On the other hand there are people who are labelled healthy even though they continue to live because of countless risky surgical interventions and aggressive treatment. Is not this distinction, between healthy and sick, an arbitrary one? Is everyone who is tired of life, because of illness or advanced age, automatically depressed and in need of psychiatric treatment? What happens when anti-depressants stop working? Does one then have to defend him from himself?

I am a gynaecologist and as such help women to give birth. I have helped many children into this world. And I have done so gladly, it has always been an act on the borders of existence, bringing someone new to the world. But it is also part of my job to terminate pregnancies, that is to destroy something that could have led a healthy life. I have done this with less enthusiasm because the decision to end pregnancy is never taken with the knowledge of the creature whose life is about to be ended.

If a person is determined to die, that does not mean he is mentally ill.

Now I am consciously active at another existential borderline, the voluntary exit from this world. I am not saying of course that suicide is the ideal resolution of a life. But it is just as legitimate as soldiering on to the natural end of a life. Both possibilities should exist—neither course is better than the other. And only those directly affected can decide on which way is the best for them.

If a person is determined to die, that does not mean he is mentally ill. Perhaps he simply does not believe in life after death and has drawn concrete conclusions.

Suicide is a human right. But it is vital not just to have that right but to be able to exercise it, with dignity and without using brutal methods. That can only occur with the medical prescription of sodium pentobarbital and with sympathetic human assistance. Suicide-help organisations make this possible.

That is why I am doing what I can to help.

12

Physician-Assisted Suicide Can Turn into a Profit Machine

Allen Hall

Allen Hall is a journalist for the Daily Mail *in London, England.*

Soraya Wernli has a mission to bring down the Swiss assisted-suicide organization Dignitas. Although philosophically amenable to assisted suicide, Wernli's experience as a nurse at Dignitas repulsed her and made her highly skeptical of the motives and ethics of the organization's founder and head, Ludwig Minelli. She also criticizes many of the doctors at the clinic who prescribe drugs for suicide. According to Wernli, Dignitas is about anything but dignity.

The black plastic bin liners were bulging and cluttered the back stairs to the office of Ludwig Minelli, founder and head of the assisted suicide organisation Dignitas.

Soraya Wernli was new to the job as a 'companion', one of those hired by Minelli, 75, to assist people in their final journey to the 'other side'.

Paperwork, words of comfort, a gentle hand for those about to end their pain-filled lives—these were some of the things the former district nurse knew she was signing up for when she agreed to work for him.

'But then, just a few days into the job, he asked me to sort through the stuff in these plastic bin liners clogging the stairs', she said.

Disrespecting the Dead

'Minelli said I should empty the sacks onto a long table—they were huge—and sort through everything. I opened one up and was horrified by what was inside. Mobile phones, handbags, ladies' tights, shoes, spectacles, money, purses, wallets, jewels.

You see these old photos of people in Nazi death camps sorting through the possessions of those who had been gassed. Well, right then and there, that is how I felt.

'I realised these were possessions which had been left behind by the dead. They had never been returned to family members. Minelli made his patients sign forms saying the possessions were now the property of Dignitas and then sold everything on to pawn and second-hand shops.

'I felt disgusted. You see these old photos of people in Nazi death camps sorting through the possessions of those who had been gassed. Well, right then and there, that is how I felt'.

A Campaign Against Dignitas

As a nurse and a former care worker for the elderly, Mrs Wernli, 51, was no stranger to death and a supporter of assisted suicide.

But in the two-and-a-half years she spent working for Minelli at his 'clinic' in Zurich, she came to believe that Dignitas was less about ethical euthanasia for the terminally ill and more of a money-making machine. Since breaking with Minelli in 2005, the mother of three has made it something of a quest to try to stop him and his killing machine.

She has launched lawsuits against him and spent . . . eight months of her time at the clinic acting as an undercover informant for the police, who were also concerned by Minelli.

Nominated for the Prize of Courage by a Swiss newspaper in 2007—she garnered praise for her efforts in exposing what she claims is a 'production line of death concerned only with profits'—Mrs Wernli has embarked on writing a book. . . .

Rushing People to Death

As a companion to those seeking to end their lives, Mrs Wernli has sat in on the suicides of 35 people. One of the first she met was Reginald Crew, 74, from Liverpool, who ended his life in the 'death house'—a residential block in Gertrudstrasse, Zurich, in January 2003.

The motor [neuron] disease sufferer was one of the first Britons to take advantage of the legal black hole which Dignitas exploits. Switzerland's liberal laws on assisted suicide suggest that [individuals] can be prosecuted [for helping someone to die] only if they are acting out of self-interest.

Minelli, a former journalist who has two daughters, has never been prosecuted for an illegal killing, but Mrs Wernli said she has seen enough to know the Swiss authorities' indifference to his practice is wrong.

Switzerland's liberal laws on assisted suicide suggest that a person can be prosecuted only if they are acting out of self-interest.

'Mr Crew arrived in the morning and was dead just hours later', she says. 'This was another of my many clashes with Minelli. I argued that it wasn't right that people land at the airport, are ferried to his office, have their requisite half-an-hour with a doctor, get the barbiturates they need and are then sent off to die.

'This is the biggest step anyone will ever take. They should at least be allowed to stay overnight, to think about what they are doing. But Minelli would have none of it. He once said to me that if he had his way, he would have vending machines where people could buy barbiturates to end their lives as easily as if they were buying a soft drink or a bar of chocolate. I support assisted suicide—but not the way he went about it'. . . .

Some Clients Were Not Terminally Ill

'I tried to be as professional and caring as possible; checking the paperwork and making sure that, above everything, those who wanted to die were suffering from a terminal illness and were not psychiatrically ill or simply tired of life'.

Eventually, Minelli was forced out to find new premises, finding a room in a business park, close to a garage and a martial arts centre. Daniel James, a young rugby player from Worcester [England], ended his life there in September last year [2008].

Just 23, Daniel had been paralysed after being crushed in a rugby scrum [scrimmage] during training, and did not want to live his life in a wheelchair.

The case caused concern both in the UK and Switzerland—but Minelli, who is also a qualified lawyer, and who knows better than most how to weave his way through the morass of opaque Swiss legislation, seems to have got away with it.

I tried to . . . [make] sure that, above everything, those who wanted to die were suffering from a terminal illness and were not psychiatrically ill or simply tired of life.

'Daniel James was by no means the first person to have been helped to die who wasn't terminally ill—and I doubt he will be the last', says Mrs Wernli.

'In March 2003, there were Robert and Jennifer Stokes from Leighton Buzzard, who were in their 50s and both had a history of mental illness and failed suicide attempts.

'They were in constant pain from chronic diseases but were not considered to be dying. Yet they were dispatched with the aid of Dignitas.

'Minelli later said that depression, in certain circumstances, can be deemed an "irreversible illness".

'This was another of my big rows with Minelli early on. I argued—and I had experience of this through my career as a nurse—that double suicides should *never* be sanctioned. One partner may want to die simply because he or she cannot cope with being alone.

'To that end, I got Minelli to agree to move one of the beds out of the death room at the Gertrudstrasse house. But I later learned that he went behind my back. Other, more un- scrupulous workers took my place to allow couples to kill themselves; one dying on the floor, the other on the bed.

'And Minelli has the cheek to call his practice Dig- nitas, when dignity is the last thing afforded to these poor people.' . . .

Working as an Informer

Zurich police confirm that Mrs Wernli became an undercover informer. For eight months she passed on information about Minelli and his practices to detectives. Then, she quietly left the clinic, without informing Minelli of her undercover role. She hasn't seen him since.

Swiss prosecutors confirm they are handling her claims about personal property being sold on and Minelli's alleged personal enrichment. Minelli denies all the allegations.

Whatever the case, Dignitas today is still in business and people are still dying. Now employees are made to sign a privacy agreement.

'Mrs Soraya Wernli quit working with Dignitas back in March 2005—almost four years ago', said a spokesman for

Dignitas. 'Thus, we wonder how she should possibly be competent to know how we work these days.

'There are, and have been, people around, who—for whatever reasons—spread rumours and false allegations. Generally, we do not comment on these rumours and allegations any more, because it is simply a waste of time.'

Whatever the case, Dignitas today is still in business and people are still dying. Now employees are made to sign a privacy agreement personally drawn up by Minelli.

Mrs Wernli has not given up. 'I like to think that some of what I passed on is still being examined by the police,' she says.

'But this is Switzerland, and things move slowly, if at all. All I can promise is that I will not stop speaking out because Dignitas is an organisation that must be stopped'.

13

End-of-Life Decisions Are Personal and Should Be Respected

John Humphrys

John Humphrys is an award-winning reporter for the British Broadcasting Corporation and the author of several books.

Modern life has changed how we grieve as well as how we view death. Grief, a deeply private experience, has become public and superficial. With modern medicine, death is farther off than it once was and not seen as a natural and often welcome part of life. One should have the same sense of self-determination when dying as one expects when living.

Rob was right to be scared. Seven weeks after [he found out] he had a tumour, he was dead. I grieve for him. What a stupidly obvious thing to write. Of course I grieve for him. He was my young brother—the little boy who had tormented me when I was a young teenager as only little boys can and then, when we'd both grown up a bit, had become my best friend. His death was a savage blow to his wife Julie, to his three children, to his many friends and to me.

As I write, Rob's face looks up at me from the cover of his brilliant autobiography, which was published a few weeks after his funeral. There is a half smile, a quizzical expression which nicely captures his approach to life—sometimes puzzled but mostly amused. I imagine, as I look at it, that there is a hint of reproach in it too. Of course, that's fanciful—the photograph was taken long before the fatal diagnosis, when he was living life to the full—but it doesn't alter the fact that I feel I let him down when he most needed me. Just as I feel I let down my father and my former wife.

Guilt in the Face of Death

Psychiatrists tell us that guilt is a common component of the grief we feel when someone who was very close to us dies. We dredge up all the things we did and said over the years that we later came to regret. We hate ourselves for having said things we should not have said and for having left unspoken so many things we should have said—especially in those final days. We are desperate to make amends when it is too late—even if there was never really anything to make amends for. Common sense dictates that there has never been a relationship between two people—however much they may have loved each other—in which it has been all sweetness and light, but common sense goes out of the window in those dark days when grief is at its most intense and the pain is most real. The guilt may be entirely irrational, but grief and reason are not natural bedfellows.

Real grief is not paraded. It is not worn like a badge. It is private.

The Loss of Private Grief

That has always been the case and I suppose it always will be, but in other ways, as our approach to death has changed over the decades, so has our approach to grief. We have largely lost the quiet, private expression of grief for those we mourn which was expressed perfectly by Wilfred Owen in his 'Anthem for Doomed Youth': 'And each slow dusk, a drawing down of blinds.' Owen was writing about another era, when tears were shed in private and dignity and reserve were displayed in public. Now it seems to have gone into reverse—perhaps because of the insatiable demands of the television cameras. Instead we have the banality of the 'How do you feel about the death of your child?' interview; the bathetic spectacle of flowers laid publicly at the spot where someone died in an accident; the collective hysteria over the death of someone we have met only in the columns of newspapers or on our television screens. When Princess Diana died it was not real grief we witnessed during that awful week of national mourning. It was mass emoting—as unhealthy and unreal as it was synthetic and orchestrated.

I was at a concert in London's Albert Hall five days after Diana's terrible accident. The main piece was to be a Mozart piano concerto. Instead, the conductor announced that it was being replaced—as a mark of respect for the dead Princess—by a requiem. Oh, and we were solemnly instructed not to applaud at the end of it. You could sense many in the audience shuffling, irritated by the change of programme and embarrassed by the whole thing, but nobody said anything. They were scared of causing offence. There is a kind of grief fascism that operates on those occasions and I find it slightly frightening. Real grief is not paraded. It is not worn like a badge. It is private.

Grief Is Part of Life

And something else has changed. When death was a natural part of life, grief was a natural part of living. Now there is a tendency to treat it as an unwelcome affliction, or the symptom of an illness which must be treated. When a child dies the other children in the school may be offered counselling, which has always struck me as both odd and potentially damaging. Left to their own devices, most children have an extraordinary ability to come to terms with tragedy. They have a way of compartmentalising, putting sad events into context, recognising that some things happen which they can do nothing about, and then getting on with their lives. Obviously there are exceptions. If their own lives are dramatically affected by the death of a parent or a sibling, that's quite different and they may well need help, but turning private grief counselling into a public industry is not the way to do it. . . .

Our ancestors would have envied us our longevity, but could not have anticipated the pain it has brought to some.

Modern Medicine Has Changed Our Attitude to Death

The attitude of modern society to death has changed because our attitude to life has changed. A century ago we knew that death was never far away and we were prepared for it. Today the opposite is true. Now our minds seem unprepared for what our bodies are doing. I am not suggesting that there should be a morbid preoccupation with death. Quite the contrary. As someone who had a new baby at an age when my grandfather would have been contemplating the end of his life I can only wonder at my good fortune. For me life did not end at sixty: a new life began. And there are many, many more like me. For that we should give thanks. God knows, I do.

Our ancestors would have envied us our longevity, but could not have anticipated the pain it has brought to some. My father lived a much longer life than most people born before the First World War and, like so many of them, became as much a victim as a beneficiary of his extra years. Medical advances meant we could keep him alive and so that is what we did—in spite of his own wishes—and the result was that his final descent into senility cast a shadow over his life. His misery was compounded by his sense that he had lost control over his life and his death. His wishes were disregarded.

Loss of Control

Rob was still in his fifties, with everything to live for, and his illness—unlike our father's—was swift and deadly. But there was one grim comparison to be made. Rob, too, felt he had lost control. His final weeks were blighted by the sense that others were making decisions for him. I had encouraged him to believe that he could beat the cancer when I should have been encouraging him to accept what we all knew was inevitable. He hated and feared what was happening to him: the ultimate loss of control and dignity. He hated it so much that he turned his face to the wall. For one dreadful period towards the end he refused to see anyone but his wife, who had to assume the role not only of comforter but also of doctor and nurse. He would allow no one else into his room.

[My brother] wanted to be in control of his own death just as he had been in control of his own life until the moment the cancer struck.

When Julie told him I was driving down to Cardiff, he told her he did not want to see me. I got in the car anyway. I was halfway down the M4 when he phoned and—in a voice I barely recognised—told me to turn back. I refused. When I walked into his bedroom he told me to leave. Again I refused. Eventually he relented and we spent the rest of the day talking.

It was a good conversation, but I did not say all the things I now wish I had said, and it was to be our last. He told me that what he wanted above all else was for everyone to leave him alone. Julie did everything humanly possible to help him through those final days, but even she could not give him the only thing he wanted. He wanted to be in control of his own death just as he had been in control of his own life until the moment the cancer struck.

Regret at the End

The day after I returned to London Rob was rushed into hospital because his lungs were filling with fluid. When I got there he was drifting in and out of consciousness. His doctor assured Julie and me that he would do nothing to try to keep him alive and he was true to his word; but it was more than twenty-four hours after Rob was admitted before the last, shuddering breath left his body.

I wish his final few days had been different. When I held his hand in his bedroom and we had our last real conversation and he told me what he feared, I wish I had been able to say to him: 'You are in control. We both know you are dying. It is for you and nobody else to decide how and when your life comes to its end. If you want help to die, we will give you that help.'

But I could not—any more than I could help my father to die—and I shall never forgive myself for that. I let them down. I believe that the dying have at least the same rights as the living: above all, the right to make their own decisions, to take control of the end of their lives in the way they wish. Anything less is a form of betrayal.

14

A Slow Death Is Better Than the Burden of Assisted Suicide

Susan Wolf

Susan Wolf is McKnight Presidential Professor of Law, Medicine, and Public Policy at the University of Minnesota and has written extensively on end-of-life care.

The author's father's battle with terminal cancer and related ailments caused him such severe suffering that he wanted to accelerate his own death. The experience of taking care of him during the final phase of his life made the author rethink, but ultimately maintain, her outspoken opposition to physician-assisted suicide and euthanasia.

My father's death forced me to rethink all I had written over two decades opposing legalization of physician-assisted suicide and euthanasia. That should not have surprised me. Years ago, when I started working on end-of-life care, he challenged my views on advance directives by insisting that he would want "everything," even in a persistent vegetative state. "I made the money, so I can spend it." More deeply, he argued that the Holocaust was incompatible with the existence of God. There is no afterlife, he claimed. This is it, and he wanted every last bit of "it" on any terms.

My father was a smart, savvy lawyer, the family patriarch. He was forceful, even intimidating at times. We had fought over the years, especially as I neared college. That was prob-

Susan Wolf, "Confronting Physician-Assisted Suicide and Euthanasia: My Father's Death," *The Hastings Center Report*, vol. 38, no. 5, September/October, 2008, pp. 23–26.

ably necessary—my separating and our disengaging. When I was a child, it was a family joke how often he and I said the same thing at the same time. We were alike in many ways.

My father was diagnosed with a metastatic [spreading] head and neck cancer in 2002. His predictable view was "spare no effort." A top head and neck surgeon worked through conflicting pathology reports to locate the primary tumor in the thyroid and excise the gland. Metastases [spreading tumorous growths] would crop up from time to time, but radiation and then CyberKnife radiosurgery kept them in check. For five years he did well.

My father was a smart, savvy lawyer, the family patriarch. He was forceful, even intimidating at times.

A Turn for the Worse

Things changed in June of 2007. The last CyberKnife treatment was billed as the worst, with significant pain likely to follow. Sure enough, ten days later, my father's pain on swallowing became severe. He began losing weight—a lot of it. He weakened. He fell twice in his apartment. His regular internist was out of town, so he went to the emergency room of a local hospital. Doctors did little for this seventy-nine-year-old man with a five-year history of metastatic thyroid cancer plus emphysema and chronic obstructive pulmonary disease.

He was briefly discharged to home but finally made it to the head and neck surgeon who had found the primary tumor in 2002. One look at my father and the surgeon admitted him, ordering a gastrostomy tube to deliver nutrition. Now my father was in an excellent hospital, with the head and neck, pulmonology, and gastroenterology services working him up. The mood brightened and the family gathered around him. I spent days in his sunny hospital room reminiscing, plowing through *The New York Times* with him, singing the college fight songs he offered as lullabies when I was little.

With multiple services focusing on my father's condition, I hoped the picture would soon come clear. I waited for a single physician to put the pieces together. And the medical picture was becoming worse. A surgical procedure revealed cancer in the liver. Pulmonology added pneumonia to the roster of lung ailments. Meanwhile, dipping oxygen saturation numbers drove a trip to the intensive care unit. Attempted endoscopy revealed a tumor between the esophagus and trachea, narrowing the esophagus. But no physician was putting the whole picture together. What treatment and palliative options remained, if any? What pathways should he—and we—be considering at this point?

With multiple services focusing on my father's condition, I hoped the picture would soon come clear. I waited for a single physician to put the pieces together.

He Said He Wanted to Stop

My father was becoming increasingly weak. He was finding it difficult to "focus," as he put it. He could not read, do *The New York Times* crossword puzzles he used to knock off in an hour, or even watch TV. Fortunately, he could talk, and we spent hours on trips he had taken around the world, family history, his adventures as a litigator. But he was confined to bed and did little when he was alone.

Then one morning he said he wanted to stop. No more tube feeding. No one was prepared for this switch from a lifetime of "spare no effort." He told me he feared he was now a terrible burden. I protested, knowing that I would willingly bear the "burden" of his illness. I suspect that what others said was more powerful, though. I was later told that the doctor urged him not to stop, warning that he would suffer a painful death, that morphine would be required to control the discomfort, and that my father would lose consciousness before the day was out. Instead of assuring my father that health professionals know how to maintain comfort after termination of artificial nutrition and hydration, my father was scared away from this option. Weeks later, my father would wish aloud that he had carried through with this decision.

Convinced now that he had no choice, my father soldiered on. But hospital personnel announced that it was time for him to leave the hospital. We were incredulous. He could not stand, walk, or eat. He had bedsores. Even transferring him from bed to a chair was difficult. And the rigors of transporting him in the early August heat were worrisome. But they urged transfer to a rehabilitation facility. My father was assured that with continued tube feeding and rehab, he could be walking into the surgeon's office in October.

My Father Was Being Abandoned

It seemed to me my father was being abandoned. His prognosis was clearly bad and he himself had now raised the prospect of stopping tube feeding [so that he could die], but it shocked me to see the hospital try to get rid of him. Yes, the hospital said he could return (somehow) in late September to see the ENT [Ear, Nose and Throat] oncologist. But as far as I knew, that physician had never even met my father. And I doubted my father would make it to September. Still, no one was integrating the big picture. There seemed to be little choice. My father was successfully transported by ambulance to another hospital with a well-regarded rehabilitation unit.

The transfer provided brief respite. My father was delighted that he was now only blocks from his apartment, and the enticing possibility of actually going home beckoned. But the rehab unit demanded hours per day of rigorous work from each patient. My father was too weak. And his pneumonia was an issue. He was moved off rehab to the medical floor. A compassionate and attentive hospitalist appeared, trying to put together the big picture. She set about collecting the reports from the prior two hospitals and integrating them. Again, many teams were on board, including rheumatology now for flaring gout.

Request for Palliative Care

I requested the palliative care team. Even though my father could be lucid and "himself," I listened painfully as he faltered through the questions on their minimental exam. It was hard to accept that this paragon of analytic and verbal precision was failing. I alerted a member of the palliative care team that my father had evidently been misinformed at the prior hospital about the consequences of stopping artificial nutrition and hydration. I urged her to find a time to reassure him that he indeed had choices, could refuse treatments if he wanted to, and could be confident that his comfort would be maintained. I made clear to her that I hoped he would choose to stay the course for now and remain with us, but that he deserved to know that he had the choice. My father had designated his two proxy decision-makers (one of them me), but could still participate in the medical decision-making. His values and his subjective experience—whether he wanted more interventions or had reached his limit—were key.

Still unresolved, though, was the question of where we were headed. Could tube feeding and rehab bring him home and even walking into the surgeon's office in October? Was there treatment that could slow the growth of the newly discovered cancer in his lung? Should we instead pursue hospice care? At times, my father's illness seemed like *Rashomon*, a story with conflicting versions and possible trajectories. But soon my father was back in the ICU [Intensive Care Unit], with oxygen saturation percentages dipping into the seventies. Tube feeding was so uncomfortable that it was administered slowly through the night. Pain medication was a constant. Despite this, he held court in his room, enjoying the banter, and offering his own with that wry smile and cocked eyebrow.

He was briefly transferred to the pulmonary care unit, as the most pressing issues at this point were actually not cancer but lung mucus and secretions, as well as pneumonia. I arrived one morning to find him upset. His nurse was not answering his calls, and his immobility left him at her mercy. I summoned the highly experienced and empathetic supervisor, but even behind closed doors with her he was afraid to speak plainly. I saw this tough-as-nails litigator reduced to fearful dependence.

Was there treatment that could slow the growth of the newly discovered cancer in his lung? Should we instead pursue hospice care?

"Can We Accelerate?"

By morning there was a new problem. My father had developed a massive bleed. Nursing had found him in a pool of his own blood, lying among the clots. The gastroenterologists took him in for a procedure, spending hours trying to find the source of the bleed. They never found it. My father required transfusion of most of his blood volume. The bleeding abated, but we knew it could resume any time.

That was it—the final blow. My father was back in the ICU now, but the bleed and the hours spent searching for its source were too much. He waited until we gathered at his bedside. His speech was halting now, but his determination obvious. "Tell me my choices." We went through each option—you can keep going like this, or you can go back to the floor if the ICU is bothering you, or you can halt the tube feeding and IV [intravenous] hydration. You also can wait, rather than deciding right now.

For close to an hour we stayed in a tight circle around his bed, straining to hear his every word, crying, responding to each question. At one point, I thought he wanted to wait, but he called us back. "It could happen again. At 2 A.M.," he said. He wanted a decision now. "That's what I want. To terminate." He made it clear he wanted to stop tube feeding and IV hydration. But that wasn't enough. He wanted consensus.

With the decision made, we set about communicating it to the caregivers and getting new orders written. It was then that he uttered three words that shook me. "Can we accelerate?" It seemed he was asking for more—a fast death, by assisted suicide or euthanasia. Reflexively, I said no, but with a promise—we can make absolutely certain they keep you comfortable. Even if you can't talk, even if you appear comatose, if you merely furrow your brow, we'll know you need more pain medication.

It seemed he was asking for more—a fast death by assisted suicide or euthanasia.

Rethinking My Opposition

I knew right away that I needed to think through my "no." In reality, we were in the ICU of a major hospital in a jurisdiction that allowed neither assisted suicide nor euthanasia. Indeed, no jurisdiction in the United States allows euthanasia, and my father was beyond assisted suicide by swallowing prescribed lethal medication, as he couldn't swallow anything. But I still needed to think this through.

I knew that in some ways, my father presented what proponents of assisted suicide and euthanasia would regard as a strong case. He was clearly dying of physical causes, unlike the controversial 1991 *Chabot* case in the Netherlands involving a patient who was merely depressed. He certainly had less than six months to live. He was probably depressed by his illness, but in a way that was appropriate to his situation. His decisional capacity had surely declined, but he was able to express definite treatment preferences.

Moreover, he wasn't asking for a change in policy or law. Statewide or national changes in policy require considering a huge range of patients, anticipating the predictable errors and abuses. The Dutch have bravely documented all of this through empirical study of their practice of legalized euthanasia—violations of the requirement for a contemporaneous request by a competent patient, doctors failing to report the practice as required, and practice falling down the slippery slope to euthanasia of newborns. Oregon has documented its experience with legalized assisted suicide, too, but only the cases reported as required, leaving great uncertainty about cases not reported. My father wasn't asking for societal change, though, only whether he himself could "accelerate." I faced the highly individual question of how to do right by my own father.

I knew in some ways my father presented what proponents of assisted suicide and euthanasia would regard as a strong case.

We Kept Vigil, Around the Clock

In truth, it was life that answered the question, not logic. In some ways, it would have been psychologically easier, or at least faster, to bring the ordeal we all were experiencing to a quick end. I was in a city far from my husband and children, doing shifts at my father's bedside at all hours, fearful of more looming medical disasters increasing his discomfort. But instead of ending all of this and fleeing, we stayed, redoubling our attention to him. I stroked his thick white hair. He and I reminisced. He was always a great raconteur. We talked and talked over the next days. The decision to stop tube feeding actually seemed to lighten his load. A decision. In a way, it was a relief.

And executing the decision took work, itself a devotion. It was around 6 p.m. when the decision was made. The ICU doctor came to the bedside to confirm the new plan and assure my father that he would be kept comfortable. But the palliative care professional, about to go off-duty, insisted that my father would need to leave the hospital. I was astonished. Was she saying he could not terminate treatment here? That the hospital had no in-patient hospice care? That you could accept invasive treatment at this hospital, but not refuse it? After years of working on end-of-life issues, I knew better. I confronted her: "You know that my father has a constitutional and common law right to refuse invasive treatment, including in this hospital." She acceded, but insisted that he would no longer meet the criteria for hospitalization; he would need to leave, to a hospice facility or home. The hospital evidently had no hospice to offer. Fine, we would set about arranging admission to hospice.

There was more—concerns over whether the fluid flowing through a remaining line would wrongly prolong his life and whether giving morphine by pump rather than through his line would do the same. I reached out by cell phone and e-mail to colleagues who were expert in maintaining comfort when artificial nutrition and hydration are stopped. We signed the papers requesting transfer to hospice. At one point, my father asked, "Will I see the end coming or fade away?" No one in the hospital was counseling my father. I worked my cell phone for answers and carried them to my father's bedside. To a man who could hold no faith after the Holocaust, I even brought the words and experience of my rabbi.

We kept vigil, around the clock. He was out of the ICU now, in a hospital room awaiting transfer to hospice. As he began to doze more and talk less, we watched carefully for the slightest sign of discomfort. We had promised we would assure his comfort. That meant constant vigilance.

The last time I saw my father, he was motionless. His eyes were closed. He had stopped speaking. He appeared unresponsive. His breathing was quieter, rasps gone with dehydration. I took his hand. I told him I loved him. I stroked his hair, still full and silvered. I spoke to him from the heart, words that remain between him and me. Then I heard myself say, "If I am a good mother, it's because you were a great father." And to my surprise, he moved his jaw. Not his lips or his mouth. But he opened his jaw three times. It was our signal, the one we'd worked out in the ICU. Three means "I-love-you." Tears streamed down my face. I struggled, remembering the rabbi's caution that the ones we love most may need permission to leave us, to die. "I know you may have to leave before I get back. That's okay." It felt nearly impossible to let him go. My chest was bursting. The pain was crushing.

When I finally left, I was working to breathe. Taking one step then another. Breaking down, collecting myself, breaking down again. He died not long after.

The ones we love most may need permission to leave us, to die.

In the End

I will not pretend—there was a price to be paid for going the longer way, not the shorter. My father died slowly. He had to trust that we would keep a ferocious vigil, demanding whatever palliative care he needed. It was he who traveled that road, not me. I paid my own price, though. I felt the heavy weight of his trust and the obligation to fight for him. I was scared I might fail. I felt very close to the jaws of death.

But with every memory we shared while he could speak, every lift of his eyebrow and wry smile, we basked together in life, reveled in a bit more of fifty-four years together and his nearly eighty on this earth. Family and caregivers did manage to keep him comfortable. He died loved and loving.

I grieve still. I reread the letters he wrote home from Oxford in his twenties, I pore over the genealogy charts he painstakingly constructed over decades, I finger the abacus he kept in his law office. I go to e-mail him, then remember. I would not want to bear the burden of having "accelerated," of causing his death by euthanasia or assisted suicide; this is hard enough. My father's death made me rethink my objections to legalizing assisted suicide and euthanasia, but in the end it left me at ease with what I've written. Staying, keeping vigil, fighting to secure a comfortable death, stroking his hair, standing guard as death approached was my duty. It was the final ripening of my love. We both changed, even closer at the end.

Organizations to Contact

The editors have compiled the following list of organizations concerned with the issues debated in this book. The descriptions are derived from materials provided by the organizations. All have publications or information available for interested readers. The list was compiled on the date of publication of the present volume; the information provided here may change. Be aware that many organizations take several weeks or longer to respond to inquiries, so allow as much time as possible.

American Foundation for Suicide Prevention (AFSP)
120 Wall Street, 22nd Floor, New York, NY   10005
Phone: (212) 363-3500 • Fax: (212) 363-6237
E-mail: inquiry@afsp.org
Web site: www.afsp.org

Formerly known as the American Suicide Foundation, the AFSP supports scientific research on depression and suicide, educates the public and professionals on the recognition and treatment of depressed and suicidal individuals, and provides support programs for those coping with the loss of a loved one to suicide. It opposes the legalization of physician-assisted suicide. The AFSP publishes educational and self-help pamphlets as well as policy statements on key issues that have an impact on suicide prevention.

American Life League (ALL)
PO Box 1350, Stafford, VA   22555
Phone: (540) 659-4171 • Fax: (540) 659-2586
E-mail: info@all.org
Web site: www.all.org

ALL is a pro-life organization that provides information and educational materials to organizations opposed to physician-assisted suicide and abortion. Its publications include pamphlets, reports, and weekly newsletters, all of which may be downloaded directly from its Web site.

American Medical Association (AMA)

515 N. State Street, Chicago, IL   60654
Phone: (800) 621-8335
Web site: www.ama-assn.org

Founded in 1847, the AMA is the primary professional association of physicians in the United States. It disseminates information concerning medical breakthroughs, medical and health legislation, educational standards for physicians, and other issues concerning medicine and health care. It opposes physician-assisted suicide. The AMA operates a library and offers many publications, including its weekly journal, *JAMA*; a weekly newspaper, *American Medical News*; and journals covering specific types of medical specialties.

American Society of Law, Medicine, & Ethics

765 Commonwealth Ave., Suite 1634, Boston, MA   02215
Phone: (617) 262-4990 • Fax: (617) 437-7596
E-mail: info@aslme.org
Web site: www.aslme.org

The society's members include physicians, attorneys, health care administrators, and others interested in the relationship between law, medicine, and ethics. The organization publishes the quarterlies *American Journal of Law & Medicine* and *The Journal of Law, Medicine & Ethics* and books such as *Legal and Ethical Aspects of Treating Critically and Terminally Ill Patients*. Its Web site hosts blogs, forums, and other interactive resources.

Compassion & Choices

PO Box 101810, Denver, CO   80250
Phone: (800) 247-7421 • Fax (866) 312-2690
Email: info@compassionandchoices.org
Web site: www.compassionandchoices.org

Compassion & Choices seeks to help individuals with end-of-life issues. They assist clients with advance directives, local service referrals, and pain and symptom management. They assert constitutional protection for aid in dying and have a team of litigators and legislative experts who work on shaping polices for end of life care, including advance directives for patients and mandates for physicians to receive pain and palliative care training. They maintain a Web archive of articles, literature, and videos.

Death with Dignity National Center (DDNC)

520 SW 6th Ave., Suite 1030, Portland, OR   97204

Phone: (503) 228-4415 • Fax: (503) 228-7454

Web site: www.deathwithdignity.org

The goal of the Death with Dignity National Center is to provide information, education, research, and support for the preservation, implementation, and promotion of Death with Dignity laws, which allow a terminally ill, mentally competent adult the right to request and receive a prescription to hasten death under certain specific safeguards. They welcome student inquiries and have educational materials available through their Web site, including an archive of their newsletter, *The Dignity Report.*

Dying with Dignity

55 Eglinton Ave. East, Suite 802, Toronto, Ontario   M4P 1G8
  Canada

Phone: (800) 495-6156 • Fax: (416) 486-5562

E-mail: info@dyingwithdignity.ca

Web site: www.dyingwithdignity.ca

Dying with Dignity is a national nonprofit organization working to improve quality of dying and to expand end-of-life choices in Canada. They advocate for improved hospice and palliative care services, as well as legislative change that will increase end-of-life care options, including physician aid-in-dying. The organization maintains a library of euthanasia-related resources.

Euthanasia Research and Guidance Organization (ERGO)

24829 Norris Lane, Junction City, OR 97448-9559
Phone and Fax: (541) 998-1873
E-mail: ergo@efn.org
Web site: www.finalexit.org

ERGO advocates the passage of laws permitting physician-assisted suicide for the advanced terminally ill and the irreversibly ill who are suffering unbearably. It seeks to accomplish its goals by providing research data, addressing the public through the media, and helping raise campaign funds. The organization's Web site contains extensive materials, including essays, frequently asked questions, a glossary of terms, and other resources.

The Hastings Center

21 Malcolm Gordon Road, Garrison, NY 10524-4125
Phone: (845) 424-4040 • Fax: (845) 424-4545
Email: mail@thehastingscenter.org
Web site: www.thehastingscenter.org

The Hastings Center is a nonpartisan research institution dedicated to bioethics and the public interest. Since 1969, the center has played a key role in raising ethical questions in response to advances in medicine, biological sciences, and social sciences. It does not take a position on such issues as euthanasia and assisted suicide but offers a forum for exploration and debate. The center publishes numerous books, papers, guidelines and journals, including *The Hastings Center Report.*

Human Life International

4 Family Life Lane, Front Royal, VA 22630
Phone: (800) 549-LIFE (5433) • Fax: 540-622-6247
E-mail: hli@hli.org
Web site: www.hli.org

Human Life International is a pro-life research, educational, and service organization. It opposes euthanasia and assisted suicide. The group publishes such books as *Death Without*

Dignity, as well as other materials. The organization's Web site provides extensive resources including their HLI commentaries, *Spirit & Life* archive, and *Mission Report* archive.

The International Task Force on Euthanasia and Assisted-Suicide

PO Box 760, Steubenville, OH   43952
Phone: (800) 958-5678
Web site: www.internationaltaskforce.org

The goal of the International Task Force is to make certain that a patient's right to receive care and compassion is not replaced by a doctor's right to prescribe lethal drugs or administer a lethal injection. The task force opposes euthanasia, assisted suicide, and policies that may threaten the lives of the medically vulnerable. It accomplishes its mission through networking, publishing materials, maintaining the Frank Reed Memorial Library, and working with lawyers in the field of bioethics. Its newsletter, the ITF *Update*, is fully archived on the organization's Web site.

The National Hospice and Palliative Care Organization (NHPCO)

1731 King Street, Suite 100, Alexandria, Virginia   22314
Phone (703) 837-1500 • Fax: (703) 837-1233
E-mail: nhpco_info@nhpco.org
Web sites: www.nhpco.org

The NHPCO is committed to improving end-of-life care and expanding access to hospice care with the goal of profoundly enhancing quality of life for dying people and their loved ones. The organization opposes euthanasia and assisted suicide. The NHPCO operates a related educational Web site, "Caring Connections," which offers extensive resources in keeping with NHPCO's mission and philosophy.

Patient Choices at End of Life—Vermont

708 Wake Robin Drive, Shelburne, VT   05482
Phone: (802) 985-9473

E-mail: info@patientchoices.org
Web site: www.patientchoices.org

Patient Choices is an advocacy organization that seeks to edu-
cate Vermonters about end-of-life options and to influence
policy, regulations, and practice that affect the terminally ill. It
works to promote the best possible pain control, palliative and
hospice care, and to enable terminally ill patients to choose
the timing and manner of dying if even the best of care fails
to prevent or alleviate unbearable suffering. The organization's
Web site provides information about its work in Vermont as
well as well links to more general articles and resources that
deal with end-of life care and assisted-death advocacy.

True Compassion Advocates
PO Box 27514, Seattle, WA   98125
Phone: (206) 366-2715
Email: eileen@truecompassionadvocates.org
Web site: www.truecompassionadvocates.org

True Compassion Advocates seeks to enhance societal support
for people who are at-risk for assisted suicide. Through education, social policy, and community action, the organization
works to oppose assisted suicide. The organization's goal is to
help patients live their lives well and painlessly until natural
death occurs. Its Web site provides extensive information on
end-of-life choices, including electronic literature, a down-
loadable brochure, and links for further research.

Bibliography

Books

Raphael
Cohen-Almagor

Euthanasia in the Netherlands: The Policy and Practice of Mercy Killing. New York, NY: Springer, 2004.

William H. Colby

Unplugged: Reclaiming Our Right to Die in America, New York, NY: AMACOM, 2006.

Jon B. Eisenberg

The Right Vs. the Right to Die: Lessons from the Terri Schiavo Case and How to Stop It from Happening Again. New York, NY: HarperCollins, 2006.

Neil M. Gorsuch

The Future of Assisted Suicide and Euthanasia. Princeton, NJ: Princeton University Press, 2009.

Rohan Hardcastle

Law and the Human Body: Property Rights, Ownership and Control. Oxford, England: Hart Publishing, 2007.

John Humphrys with Sarah Jarvis

The Welcome Visitor: Living Well, Dying Well. London, England: Hodder & Stoughton, 2009.

Nancy S. Jecker, Robert A. Pearlman, and Albert R. Jonsen

Bioethics: An Introduction to History, Methods and Practice. Sudbury, MA: Jones and Bartlett Publishers 2007.

Sharon R. Kaufman	*And a Time to Die: How American Hospitals Shape the End of Life.* New York, NY: Scribner, 2005.
Stephen Kiernan	*Last Rights: Rescuing the End of Life from the Medical System.* New York, NY: St. Martin's Press, 2006.
John B. Mitchell	*Understanding Assisted Suicide: Nine Issues to Consider.* Ann Arbor, MI: University of Michigan Press, 2007.
David Novak	*The Sanctity of Human Life.* Washington, DC: Georgetown University Press, 2009.
Barry Rosenfeld	*Assisted Suicide and the Right to Die: The Interface of Social Science, Public Policy, and Medical Ethics.* Washington, DC: American Psychological Association, 2004.
Wesley J. Smith	*Forced Exit: Euthanasia, Assisted Suicide and the New Duty to Die.* New York, NY: Encounter Books, 2006.
Mary Warnock and Elisabeth Macdonald	*Easeful Death: Is There a Case for Assisted Dying?* New York, NY: Oxford University Press, 2009.

Periodicals

| Jacob M. Appel | "Next: Assisted Suicide for Healthy People," *Huffington Post*, July 16, 2009. |

Charles Bentz — "Don't Follow Oregon's Lead—Say No to Assisted Suicide," *Calgary Herald*, January 17, 2009.

Hal Bernton — "Washington's Initiative 1000 Is Modeled on Oregon's Death with Dignity Act," *Seattle Times*, October 13, 2008.

Gillian Bowditch — "The Dangers of Dicing with Assisted Death," *Sunday Times*, May 3, 2009.

Paige Bowers — "Final Exit: Compassion or Assisted Suicide," *Time*, March 2, 2009.

Jane E. Brody — "A Heartfelt Appeal for a Graceful Exit," *New York Times*, February 5, 2008.

Tim Christie — "A Gift of Treatment," *Register-Guard*, June 3, 2008.

Steve Doughty — "I've Changed My Mind, Says Woman in Right-to-Die Case," *Daily Mail*, April 19, 2007.

Bruce Fein — "Bogus Federalism," *Washington Times*, June 1, 2004.

Marie Jeanne Ferrari — "Is There an Alternative to Euthanasia," *Catholic Insight*, November, 2008.

Ilora Finlay — "Assisted Suicide Is Fine in a Perfect World. We Don't Live (or Die) in One," *Times* (London), April 1, 2009.

Herbert Hendin
and Kathleen
Foley

"Physician-Assisted Suicide in
Oregon: A Medical Perspective," *The
Michigan Law Review*, June 2008.

Stephen
Hutchison

"Legalising Euthanasia Needs Careful
Thought," *Inverness Currier*,
December 23, 2008.

Barbara
Coombs Lee

"AMA Opposition and the Path
Ahead," *Huffington Post*, June 17,
2009.

Rita L. Marker

"An Open Letter to Baroness
Warnock on Assisted Suicide,"
American Thinker, October 4, 2008.

Christina
Nicolaidis

"My Mother's Choice," *Journal of the
American Medical Association*, August
23, 2006.

George Tibbits

"11 End Lives Under WA Assisted
Suicide Law," Associated Press,
September 8, 2009.

Sam Vaknin

"Euthanasia and the Right to Die,"
Associated Content, June 27, 2007.

Index